Keep Your Clothes on!
There's More *Gauntlet* To Come

Remember, now 2 issues of *Gauntlet* a year - May and November. Don't miss an issue. #7 focuses on Prostitution Subscribe now!

Issue #7 - $9.95 + $2 p&h
One year (issues #7 & #8)
$18 + $4 p&h

#2 Stephen King Special with King's "The Dreaded X" on film censorship, 40-pages devoted to the Master of Horror, plus 2 Live Crew, Kiddie Porn, "Outing" - 402-pp $10.95

#3 Politically (In)Correct Issue with Wm. M. Gaines' last comprehensive interview, rape and sexual harassment by US soldiers during the Persian Gulf War, expanded comics section, and 57-pages on the mnd control of politically correct - 336-pp. $12.95

#4 Media Manipulation with media pandering to Black cultists, gays and the mainstream press, political manipulation of the media, serial card controversy - 176-pp. $9.95

#5 Porn in the USA, debating the pros and cons of pornography with Nina Hartley, Annie Sprinkle, Candida Royalle against the likes of Phyllis Schlafly and Jim Bramlett; plus exposes on Spike Lee and Madonna and an original *Omaha the Cat Dancer* - 192-pp. $9.95

T-shirts from our Stephen King issue are available and make great holiday gifts, along with back issues or a subscription to *Gauntlet*.
Order now for immediate delivery!

GAUNTLET Exploring The Limits Of Free Expression

ANYTHING GOES

COMIC CENSORSHIP

FICTION

REVIEWS

Published by *Gauntlet*, Inc.
Barry Hoffman, President

Founder/Editor-in-Chief
  Barry Hoffman

Editorial Consultant
  R. M. Hoffman

Assistant to the Editor
  David Reed

Circulation Manager
  Cheryl Meyer

Research Assistant
  Dara Lise, D. Kingsley Hahn,
  Barbara McDonald

Columnists
  Richard G. Carter

Layout and Design
  Kara Tipton

Cover Editor
  Leslie Sternbergh

Cover Photo
  Adam Alexander of Seaton
  B. Hancock

Front Cover Layout
  Mark Michaelson

Editorial Cartoons
  Andy Wahl, George Gehlert,
  John Bergstrom, Russ Miller,
  Keith Towler, Russ Miller

Gauntlet wishes to thank F.O.X.E.
Freedom Wall contributors: F. Jones,
Joseph H. March, Carter Churchill,
Frank W. Redmon & James E. Gates

Address all letters/queries/orders
to: *Gauntlet*, Dept. B93, 309 Powell
Rd., Springfield, Pa. 19064

Advertising Rates: Full page — $400;
Half Page — $250; Quarter Page —
$175; Inside Covers — $500

Subscriptions: *Gauntlet* is published
twice a year in November and May.
One year (2 issues) subscription is
$20 plus $2 p&h. Canadian Orders
add $4 postage per issue; Foreign
Orders add $7 postage per issue.
Checks made payable to *Gauntlet*,
Inc. sent to the above address. **U.S.
Funds Only.**

Back Issues: Issues #2, #3, #4 & #5
are available in limited quantities.
Send $10.95 for issue #2, $12.95 for
issue #3, and $9.95 for issues #4 & #5
plus $2 p&h for **each** issue, payable
to *Gauntlet*, Inc. to the above address.
A limited quantity of the hardcover
Stephen King limited, signed by
Stephen King and over 20 other contributors is available. Query Barry
Hoffman, with SASE for details.

GAUNTLET CORRESPONDENTS:
Gauntlet seeks journalists/investiga-
tive reporters from around the country willing to track down and
investigate stories dealing with censorship and free expression issues.
Query with SASE.

ARTISTS/CARTOONISTS: *Gauntlet* seeks artists and cartoonists. Send
samples of your work to be kept on
file to Cheryl Meyer, at the above
address. Enclose SASE for response.

ADVERTISING EXECUTIVE:
Gauntlet seeks an advertising executive, to be paid with a generous commission. Work from your home.
Query with resume and SASE.

Printed in the U.S.A.

EDITORIAL MEANDERINGS

Oddly enough there was little overt censorship of issue #5, "Porn in the USA." We feared the worst and were surprised that censors allowed us in their doors. For example, we had no trouble entering Britain, even with an original Omaha the Cat Dancer strip. You see, Omaha has had trouble getting past customs, yet we got through. Go figure. We were booted out of a Barnes and Nobles in Bountiful Utah (probably others, but this is the only one we can document), and we spoke to the magazine buyer to find out why. He explained that he'd received too much pressure from the Mormons over sexually-oriented material and he was tired of them yelling in his face. He stocks a few copies of Playboy and Penthouse under the counter, but without name recognition he wasn't prepared to go to bat for us. Just as disturbing, a Minneapolis store carried Gauntlet, but in a plastic envelope. Again, without name recognition readers must be allowed to page through an issue; an impossibility when wrapped in plastic.

While our focus topic for #6 is Black Racism, this issue contains a potpourri of material covering invasion of privacy, government forfeiture, the new battle political plan of the religious right, additional articles on porn and erotic art.

It has become evident that sex is the last frontier, in this country, as regards censorship. With all the talk about lessening the level of violence on television, it is forgotten that sex still is forbidden fruit; it's not even open to debate. Films receiving the dreaded NC-17 rating invariably involve too much sex. Snip a few seconds here and there and you get the preferred R. On television the new Stephen Bochco series NYPD Blue has run afoul of affiliates because of sex (precious little) and profanity. There is a great deal of implied sex on the tube, but on network television sex (as in naked men and women) is where a firm line is drawn in the sand. Watching a show like Entertainment Tonight, which oh-so-cleverly uses banners to cover breasts and genitals, as they lure an audience by seemingly getting down and dirty, would be laughable if it were not so hypocritical.

For this reason, we have decided to profile erotic artists in all future issues; possibly devote a focus topic to erotic art. For starters we would try to define the difference between what's erotic and what's pornographic. As neither has a legal definition, it seems to be in the eye of the beholder. What's erotic to one is most definitely pornographic to another. That's for another issue. For now our profiled artists have stories to tell about self-censorship and imposed censorship. We're most definitely interested in your reaction.

Our next issue, available in May, will focus on prostitution, with a guest editor who is herself a former prostitute. If you want to participate in the debate, please query (with a SASE). We're also interested in cults and further stories of abuse of forfeiture laws.

Enough already. Read, enjoy and prepared to be aggravated by the many viewpoints expressed.

Barry Hoffman
August 1993

This issue is dedicated to my father, Robert Hoffman, who passed away in April of this year. He was a constant source of inspiration and as a father was "Simply the Best."

OPENERS

Seeking Information?

We have received mail requesting a list of organizations combatting censorship. For any number of reasons, we are reluctant to run such a list. *Gauntlet* will not endorse an organization solely because it purports to oppose censorship. At the same time we feel an obligation to let readers know where such information is available. The Free Expression League began publishing a quarterly anti-censorship newsletter in August, which provides an updated listing of anti-censorship groups. Send 2 stamps to P.O. Box 436, New Philadelphia, OH 44663 for a free sample.

Know Your Enemies

We received the following anonymously (we're always suspicious when something arrives anonymously; like someone has something to hide), postmarked Paterson, NJ. We run the following "message" as a public service, as to combat bigots, censors and zealots one must know your enemy. Here's one opportunity.

Pros and Cons

Cons

Anti-abortionists are using a new tactic in Melbourne, FL: 10-14 year-old children paraded outside an abortion clinic, violating a court order, while their parents watched behind police barricades across the street. As to be expected, none were arrested, but were detained and released to their parents. If you can't stand the heat, parents, get out of the damn kitchen.

Pros

Two Penn State students were arrested for stealing 4000 copies of the conservative-slanted *The Lionhearted* because they were offended by the papers lambasting of women's groups. One of the women, co-director of Womyn's Concerns said *The Lionhearted*'s distribution violated university anti-discrimination codes. The thieves, she said, "simply removed the source of the pain." Unlike other schools, like the University of Penn, police took a dim view of the theft even if it wasn't the politically correct thing to do.

Cons

To Walt Disney Co. for acceding to the demands of the American-Arab Discrimination League and altering the words to all future versions of the song "Arabian Nights" from the classic *Aladdin*; the most commercially successful animated film of all time. The offending verse:

> Where they cut of your eye
> If they don't like your face
> It's barbaric, but hey it's home

changed to

> Where it's flat and immense
> And the heat is intense
> It's barbaric, but hey it's home

Lyricist Howard Ashman had no say in the matter. He's passed away and approval was obtained from his estate. One wonders whether theater groups would agree to change offensive language from a Shakespeare play, for example, because it was *now* not politically correct? And given so many advocacy groups, one cringes at the thought of the havoc they could wreak if groups like Disney continue to buckle under to the pressure of special interest groups.

Pros

One video store owner in St. Louis has gone against the tide and is restocking adult X-rated films to its shelves. The owner, who wished to remain anonymous for fear of harassment, feels the city's new prosecutor won't target pornography as readily as predecessor George Peach. Peach, by the way, resigned in disgrace after allegations "he took cash from public checks before assignations and used city money to buy at least one sex tape." (One wonders where?) Kudos, too, to new prosecutor Dee Joyce-Haynes saying she "wouldn't focus the limited resources of her office on pornographic tapes." (BM)

Cons

The interracial kiss between Michelle Pfeiffer and Dennis Haysbert in *Love Field* was excised from an airline version of the flick. The reason, according to an Orion film spokesperson was to save time. The length of the kiss, *Newsweek* reports, was 3 seconds. (DKH)

Pros

To prospective security guards whose suit forced Target stores to agree to a $1.3 million settlement when the applicants objected to a psychological test they felt was an invasion of privacy. A sampling of questions (all true and false):

I feel sure there is only one true religion.

I have had no difficulty starting or holding my bowel movement.

Evil spirits possess me sometimes.

I believe my sins are unpardonable.

I am very strongly attracted by members of my own sex.

Cons

Pressure from Vietnamese-American groups have led to the cancellation of a nationally touring exhibit at the Minneapolis Museum of Art dealing with the war in Vietnam. *As Seen By Both Sides: American and Vietnamese Artists Look at the War* is a 2 1/2 year-old show which had successfully toured 13 cities and shows the paintings of Americans (many of them veterans) alongside their former-Communist enemies. Tri D. Nguyen in denouncing the show claimed "These paintings will only reopen deep wounds that have been felt by both Americans and Vietnamese . . . " (DKH)

Cons

Money talks: For the first time, *The Donahue Show* this May acknowledged it had opened its wallet to the tune of $25,000 apiece to snare two defendants from the Rodney King trial. Even more dismaying, as a result, the two, Theodore Briseno and Stacey Koon, backed out of interviews they had agreed to do for *free* on *Today* and *CBS This Morning*.

Pros

Also in May (can you say "sweeps"), David Thibodeau, a survivor of the Branch Davidian cult compound blaze canceled a *Nightline* appearance to appear on *A Current Affair*. A *Nightline* spokesman told the *Dallas Morning News* the show was asked whether it wanted to make a better offer than *A Current Affair*. "We refused . . . We will not pay a guest for an appearance on any ABC news program." *Nightline*'s stand is to be applauded.

Cons

If the Minnesota legislature has its way Minneapolis and St. Paul will be able to reinstitute the confiscation of cars of suspected prostitution customers. The "Johns Sweep" had been declared unconstitutional by a Minnesota Court of Appeals which led the legislature to take up the cause. Before the St. Paul ordinance was invalidated police in 6 sweeps had arrested 110 johns and seized 90 vehicles for forfeiture proceedings. One representative, overruled by his colleagues, called confiscating a $10-20,000 car "overkill" for a crime that's only a misdemeanor. (DKH)

A similar statute was proposed but defeated by the St. Petersburg City Council. Hold the praise, though. In May, the same council passed an ordinance mandating that the names and addresses of convicted johns be broadcast on local government access TV. Names have already been broadcast and a police spokesman reported prostitution solicitation has decreased immediately as a result. A new meaning to the phrase "By any means necessary." (CG)

Cons

Snow White bit the dust in Jacksonville, FL where it was regarded as too violent for Kindergarten-2nd graders. One offending section: "And when a young boar suddenly sprang into view, the hunter stabbed him, removed his lungs and liver and brought them to the Queen. She had them salted and cooked, and the wicked woman ate them up, believing she had eaten Snow White's liver and lungs."

Cons

If you can't close a strip joint one way . . . An obscenity ordinance approved in Silver Springs, MO may effectively end semi-nude dancing there. The ordinance, among other things, prohibits tipping dancers which prevents them from making more than the minimum wage. One owner who employs about 30 full-time or part-time dancers asked, "Who are we hurting? Nobody's forced to come in here."

A week later Blondies became the first such bar to cave in and close. The bar's attorney said it would be less costly to close than to fight the ordinance in court (We know, you're asking where was the ACLU? Could be they avoid sex like the plague). His argument was that dancers could not be denied tips when waitresses and bartenders in the same establishment were allowed to receive them. Good point, but without a legal challenge one that is moot. (BM)

Cons

Sexual harassment gone awry in Fairfax County, VA where Thomas Sowell tells of a 20-year veteran teacher who committed suicide after being fired for sex harassment. The 280-pound teacher, who often poked fun at his weight, apparently encouraged give and take (all in good fun) between himself and his students. One girl made a kidding remark about how big his chest was and he retorted that hers was small. Sex harassment charges were brought, he was dismissed and killed himself.

---

*Thanks to D. Kingsley Hahn, Barbara McDonald and Cecil Greek for contributing information to this section. Blurbs such as these do not make national news. If your local paper prints such an incident, please send a copy to **Gauntlet** for consideration.*

WHITE TO WHITE ON BLACK/WHITE
by Toni E. Weaver, Ph.D.

Finally, a cause and effect approach to help whites understand racism in America!

This is a 112-page handbook that is educational and motivational and translates doctoral research into an easy to read format that addresses whites' most often asked questions on race relations, such as:

-**Why** are Blacks so angry?
-**Why** not just hire the best qualified?
-**Kind** should stick to kind, shouldn't they?
-**Is** is true that Black men are bigger (or better)?
-**Isn't** prejudice getting less with each generation?

Practical solutions to become a part of the solution in eliminating racism are offered as well as additional recommended reading.

TO ORDER, please send check or money order for $12.00 to:

VOICES PUBLISHING, P.O. BOX 13-GD, VANDALIA, OH 45377

NAME_____

ADDRESS_____

CITY/STATE/ZIP_____

SELECTIVE OUTRAGE

Joseph Perkins

No one slept in on the Saturday morning the verdict was returned in the Rodney King beating trial. Not since Neil Armstrong became the first man to set foot on the moon have so many Americans sat so anxiously by their television sets.

It should have been an open-and-shut police brutality case, handled in the manner of the dozen or so excessive force complaints that the Los Angeles Police Department logs every year. But once the racial element was introduced, the case took on a life all its own. The first trial ended in acquittals, which touched off last spring's riots. A similar verdict the second time around was expected to ignite no less than a race war.

I do not know whether the savage beating Rodney King received at the hands of four white police officers was motivated by his complexion. But what I do know is that if the black motorist had been similarly beaten by black officers, we would not have heard the same hue and cry — it just would have been four black cops who roughed up a fleeing felon.

This selective outrage is one of the great hypocrisies of the black community. When white victimizes black there is protest. The churches are packed. The streets are filled. But . . . when black victimizes black there is silence. The pews are empty, the streets vacant.

The explanation of this phenomenon is that black-on-black crime has no political currency. It cannot be traded upon the way that white-on-black crime can.

As long as black Americans can be portrayed as victims of societal or institutional injustice, we can make claims on the system. So it was that the Rodney King case became a pretext for the black community to mau-mau for more government aid and private philanthropy.

To listen to Jesse Jackson, Benjamin Chavis and other prominent black leaders in the wake of the King verdict, one almost came away with the impression that America had returned to the days when black lynchings were commonplace.

"It makes me weep to think that we have to always continually go through this much drama to get some justice," said a misty-eyed Jackson. "We've learned when you get some justice, you have to fight for the rest," said a defiant Chavis.

But here's the dirty little secret that the black leadership is unwilling to speak about: The prospect of a black being physically attacked by a white is far less likely than a black being killed — not just

> " . . . when black victimizes black there is silence. The pews are empty, the streets vacant."

assaulted — by a person of his own race.

Consider that in 1992, the FBI reported 1,689 racially motivated attacks against blacks. This number is troubling, but not nearly so profoundly as the 8,000 or so black homicides last year, roughly 95 percent of which were committed by other blacks.

Whenever there is a so-called hate crime against a black person, it is treated as front-page news. If it is sensational enough, maybe Jesse and Ben will come to town. But when there is a black-on-black murder, the story is relegated to the back pages, if that. It is too routine an occurrence to rate more than a passing notice.

What message does this send? It says to me that black life is deemed less valuable when it is taken by an-other black than when it is threatened by a white. This is backward. The threat of a black being victimized by a white is fairly remote. The chances of blacks falling prey to one of their own is 10 times greater.

Just visit South Central Los Angeles or south Dallas or southeast Washington, D.C. The black residents of these neighborhoods are afraid to move about. They fear that if they stop at a traffic light, they might be rousted from their car by a "jacker". That if they stand on the wrong corner, they might catch an errant bullet from a drive-by shooting.

The black inner cities have become urban jungles and young black males the predators. While black men aged 15 to 24 constitute 1 percent of the U.S. population, they com-

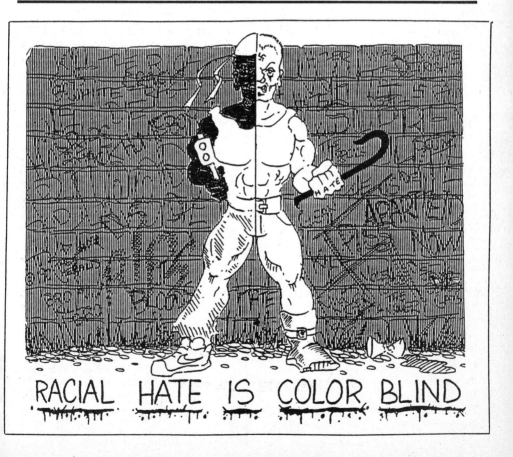

RACIAL HATE IS COLOR BLIND

mit 19 percent of the nation's murders. A young black man growing up in the ghetto has a better chance of dying from a bullet than from heart disease, auto accidents, suicide or cancer — the leading causes of death for virtually every other segment of the population.

There are some black leaders who would attribute intraracial crime to social and economic factors, for which whites ultimately are responsible. Were young black men not reared in poverty, the argument goes, were jobs readily available to them, were they not victims of racism, they would not bend toward crime.

But social and economic conditions for young black men in 1993 are hardly worse than they were for their fathers and grandfathers. Yet, no generation of black men in American history has been as violent as those who currently hold the nation's inner cities under siege.

Before Rodney King was elevated by the black community to the status of Rosa Parks and Martin Luther King, he was just another potential predator. He had already been convicted of knocking off a convenience store. With his drug habit and alcohol abuse, there is no telling what crimes to which he may have graduated.

The black community was prepared to protest, to riot even, if justice was not served in the King beating trial, if all four white officers were exonerated of using excessive force against the black man. Meanwhile, nary a voice is raised in sympathy to the thousands of blacks who lose their lives year by year at the hands of their violent young men.

Joseph Perkins is a columnist for The San Diego Union-Tribune

THE RODNEY KING TRIAL: A POSTLOGUE

Steven Barnes

Today, Monday, Los Angeles is breathing easier, because two police officers by the names of Stacy Koon and Laurence Powell were declared "guilty" in the climax of the most heavily publicized legal case in American history.

Last year, a "not-guilty" verdict triggered a riot that left at least 52 dead and resulted in more than a billion dollars in property damage. Not only that, but it ripped open what many thought to be the healed scar tissue from four hundred years of violent and hateful race relations in America.

What does it all mean? Who is right? Who is wrong? The images of four police officers beating the holy hell out of an apparently defenseless man shocked the world. What can be said about this?

In the past year more, and uglier, questions have been asked concerning race relations in America than in the twenty years previous. In all probability the questions boil down into four basic categories:

1) Were the five Foothill PD officers correct in their actions?
2) Why did the riots happen?
3) Why can't black people seem to get their act together?

4) Hasn't anything changed for the better vis a vis racism in America?

It has caused me so much pain to listen to all of the controversy, wondering about it all, and thinking it through, that perhaps it is time for me to put my thoughts down in print. GAUNTLET has offered a forum, which I gratefully accept.

Let's take the questions in numerical order, and see if we can come to any useful conclusions.

1) Were the five Foothill PD officers correct in their actions? In my opinion, no, and I'll explain that in a moment. On the other hand, were those actions understandable? Yes, and I'll explain that too.

The question of "correctness" has to do with two things: was it a legal use of force, and was it the minimum amount of force necessary to subdue Rodney King? Well, the court decided it was an illegal use of force, but then an earlier jury decided it wasn't. The fact of the racial makeup of the first jury (10 Caucasians, 1 Oriental, 1 Latino) as opposed to the second jury (9 Caucasians, 2 African-Americans, 1 Latino) may well have had something to do with it. After all, If the jury had been composed of 10 African-Americans, 1 Oriental, and 1 Latino, I would have equal doubts that a fair trial could be conducted. Why? Because in my view, racial prejudice is hard-wired into the human nervous system. Our intellect works primarily to tell us what is similar to, or dissimilar to, a given object or situation. And color is one of the easiest ways to differentiate.

The extraordinary thing is that so many intelligent, sensitive, caring people manage to rise above these base tendencies. Their effort and continual striving give me hope for humanity.

But, you might ask, wasn't that original jury mixed? Not in any realistic sense. Remember: Asians do not consider themselves to be of the same social class or quality as Blacks. Neither do Latinos. In essence, you had a jury that was composed completely of people who might well consider themselves superior to African-Americans. Is it not predictable that such a jury might lean in the direction of acquittal?

Why? Because the "thin blue line" which protects the "honest folks" from the "dishonest ones" also protects the Desirables from the Undesirables.

> "I can guarantee you that it does not take 56 baton blows to subdue an unarmed human being."

As a black man, I can tell you in no uncertain terms that I must continually earn my position as one of the "Desirables". I believe that African-Americans must do this continually. Whites, on the other hand, are born into the class of desirables (at least in a racial sense) and must "fall out of it" by breaking the law, sporting long hair, acting effeminate, carrying unpopular political placards, etc. Then the minions of law and order might well judge them to be "undesirable."

As to the question of minimum force . . . well, I don't know much about politics, and I don't know much about our legal system. But I have studied martial arts for almost 25 years, including 3 years of Filipino stick fighting. I can guarantee you that it does not take 56 baton blows to subdue an unarmed human being. If the officers involved honestly believed that it did, then they were either criminally stupid or hideously maltrained.

If their training was not at fault, and they knew how to subdue him in less time and with less violence, then they were simply administering rough justice, as cops have probably done since the time of the Roman Centurions. Rodney King fled from them and then shook his ass at them. Their adrenaline was up, and they were pissed. So they beat the hell out of him. Probably happens every day, a very human response. Would they do it to a white man? Sure, if he had long hair, drove a VW with a Fuck the Pigs bumper sticker, acted stoned, or otherwise demonstrated that he wasn't a card-carrying member of the power structure. But remember — in a racial sense, a white person is automatically a member of the power structure until proven otherwise, whereas a black one is automatically not, until proven otherwise. So, statistically speaking, probably more black skulls are still cracked to this day. Certainly huge numbers of black people believe this.

Ignore their belief if you will — but to do that you have to say that all them black folks is just lyin', and by doing so you are probably saying more about yourself than about them black folks.

So: Either these were good men but bad cops, or good cops but bad men. But what they could not conceivably have been is both good cops and good men. End of story.

2) Why did the riots happen?

First of all, understand that there were two distinct phases to the riots. 1) The first 2-3 hours. 2) The period thereafter.

In one sense, the first 180 minutes or so were the "Blasting Cap", which set off a bundle of social "dynamite." This "Blasting Cap" consisted of shock, fear, anger, and righteous indignation. The "Dynamite", on the other hand, was opportunistic criminal behavior.

Basically, after the controversial "not-guilty" verdict, thousands of people went temporarily insane. Why?

Well, please understand the history of African-Americans. For the first three hundred years of their presence, they could be — and were — raped, tortured and murdered without any legal protection from their tormentors. After emancipation, they still did not have full legal rights, and it wasn't until the Civil Rights Amendment passed in the 1960's that it could be said that Apartheid truly ended in America. Now, then. During all of that time, the popular mythology was that white men could and did kill, beat, and torture black men, and that they were over and over again judged innocent by all-white juries.

Read your histories of the civil rights movement, and you will find far too many nauseating examples of just this sort of perfidy. But has it ended? For decades African-Americans have claimed that heads were still being busted in the inner city, and nobody listened. Literally every black man I know has had a run-in with the police which, at least subjectively, seemed racially motivated. Some were mild, some were hideously violent. But literally EVERY Black man that I've ever talked to about this agrees. And White people simply refuse to believe it.

So when Rodney King got pulled over, and his subsequent head-whipping actually got VIDEOTAPED, for the first time in history there seemed to be irrefutable evidence of what we'd been saying all along: that white men beat the hell out of black men under the color of authority, with no fear of legal reprisals.

When the "Not-guilty" verdict came back, (whether or not it was, in this instance, justified) there was a public perception that the justice system still operated in that racist mold. White men beating black men, being judged and exonerated by white people.

What resulted was a blast of naked, seething fear, hatred, resentment, and anger. For a few hours it felt as if the world had fallen apart, and all of the institutions we had been taught to trust had worked against us. The same old story. Our lives were forfeit at the whim of any passing white man, and there was nothing we could do to protect ourselves. For God's sake — the officers claimed that "every twitch or attempt of Rodney King to protect himself from their blows could be interpreted as an aggressive act"!!!!!!

Does anyone really believe that if those had been four black cops beating a white man, judged by an all-white jury, that they would have gotten off? Does anyone believe that if they had been judged in Watts by an all-black jury and exonerated, there wouldn't have been violence? Not on the same scale, certainly. What you have to factor in is that Anger is fear turned inside out. And Blacks have far more to fear from Whites than Whites have to fear from Blacks — we are horribly outnumbered, and exist within a social structure which kept us helpless for four hundred years. The last legal barri-

ers were only removed in the late Sixties. In other words, for 100 years following emancipation, millions of white people failed to exhibit simple decency and respect for the law. Who in the hell are they to expect black people to adjust three times faster???

2) The violence which followed the first three hours was simple criminal opportunism. Thugism. Mob rule. Inexcusable. These people need to do hard time. The people who exploded in the beginning, assuming they had no prior arrests, could possibly be judged more lightly (with the exception of the bastards who dragged Reginald Denny from his truck). When, as a child, I watched Whites beating and siccing dogs on Blacks in Selma Alabama, bombing Black churches, lynching little Black boys and murdering Freedom Riders, I never thought they were representative of all White people. I thought they were representative of human fear and anger. When people feel threatened, as southern Whites did by the emergence of a changing social order, violence often results. It has always been that way, and may always be that way. What we need is better communication between individuals.

3) Why can't Black people seem to get their act together?

I love this question. It is usually followed by some specious comparison between Blacks and Italian or German immigrants. Or Vietnamese immigrants. "These other groups have done so well, and African Americans have these problems with crime, and illiteracy, and drugs . . . "

Well, let me demolish the central argument first. There is absolutely no comparison between African-Americans who are descended from slaves, and European or Asian Immigrants. If you want to make an immigrant comparison, then you must compare European immigrants, Asian immigrants and African immigrants. To my knowledge, African immigrants perform about as well as any others.

Why are the descendants of slaves different? If you need that answered, you aren't quite as intelligent as you think you are. African-Americans were completely shorn of their names, languages, history, religion, cultural identity, mythology, and tribal heritage. Human beings without culture are as helpless as any lessor primate. Instead of being "People of African descent and culture living in America," Black people are culturally adrift, attempting to create our own culture out of environmental scraps. As individuals Blacks are as intelligent, creative, and potentially successful as anyone. As a group, however, we exhibit some extreme pathologies.

Almost every white person I know can trace his or her history back to "the old mother country." Every Asian I know can identify where his or her ancestors came from. Not a single African-American I know can do the same.

White Christians kneel in church to a deity which is personified as a man of their own skin color. They cannot even imagine what it would be like to kneel to a Black god. Every day of their lives Whites have been surrounded with pictures of themselves as sexy, intelligent, successful, conquering demigods. Virtually every dramatic television show or heroic film emphasizes this. UNCOUNTED MILLIONS of such images in comic books, billboards, television shows, plays, movies, magazines, textbooks, and on and on and on.

Asians, although cheated of these benefits AS AMERICANS, still had their cultural stories, their history, their family names, their mythology, their language. They could go to theaters in their neighborhood (in every Chinatown, and every Little Tokyo) and see heroic, sexual, success-oriented images of themselves.

The only people in America cut off from such cultural strength are African-Americans. And I believe that uncounted billions of dollars are invested in such books, movies, television shows, etc. because heroic images are an essential emotional nutrient. They help a young man, or a young woman answer the question: Who am I? What does it mean to fail? What does it mean to confront evil, or hatred?

Without these questions answered countless times, in the metaphor of Jesus Christ, Rambo, Spider-Man, Batman, John Wayne, or Steven Segal, little boys don't quite understand how in the world they will ever grow up to take their place in the world.

You might point out that little girls don't have these images either — but little girls don't want the exact thing that little boys want. Most of the women I know feel repulsed by the very cinematic images of power, violent conquest and success that make little boys drool.

Little black boys, on the other hand, want pretty much the exact same things that little white boys want. They simply aren't shown any routes to attain them.

Why do you think that so many young black men want to get into sports? Because sports is the only arena where African-Americans are allowed to be fully functioning men: conquering, sexual, smart, cocky. They can strut their stuff, and literally crush a White opponent into the dust without being arrested or killed for doing it.

In the late forties, television began to create a mass popular culture. For the first time in history, one group — upper class White males — created the mythology for the entire culture.

And guess what that mythology said about Black men? They were sexless, stupid, criminal nothings.

It is a rare White person indeed who can understand the hunger Black America felt for the image of Bill Cosby in I Spy, or Greg Morris in Mission Impossible. And the first image of a Black man truly standing up for his humanity came as late as 1967, in *In The Heat of the Night*, when Sidney Poitier slapped a White man in self-defense.

But before then, little White boys had been treated to uncounted thousands of images of images of Tarzan killing dozens of gibbering black natives, Butterfly McQueen whining that she didn't "know nothin' 'bout birthin' no babies, Miz Scarlett", and James Bond telling his black companion to "Fetch my boots."

Ugh.

Do I really think mythological images make that much difference? Friend, do you really think I would be spending my entire life energy writing fiction if I didn't??

4) Hasn't anything changed for the better vis a vis racism in America?

Of course it has. And only an ignoramus, or one with a political axe to grind, would say otherwise.

My father, who was a backup singer for Nat King Cole, couldn't walk in the front door of hotels where he performed for the pleasure of White audiences. My mother, who was very light skinned, was mistaken for White often enough to cause real problems when they traveled together. For instance, my father wasn't allowed to sit down and eat food that my mother had ordered in a restaurant, once the management realized that they had been "tricked into serving Negroes." My father was forced to pay for food he wasn't allowed to eat.

That was the way of the world a generation ago. It ain't now. Racism has become far subtler, and less powerful — but it still exists.

On both sides.

It is regrettable that filmmakers like Spike Lee become icons. Unchallenged, they say things that would get a White filmmaker boycotted. He considers all White women unattractive? What would happen if Woody Allen said he considered all Black women unattractive? I use the comparison deliberately. In my mind, they are two sides of the same coin: brilliant, neurotic, bigoted little men.

Woody Allen, on the other hand, can hide his xenophobia merely by remaining within the very narrow social milieu he has mined for a quarter-century. How many White people have even noticed that non-Caucasians never appear in his movies except as non-Caucasians. In other words, a black woman will appear in *Bananas* so that a joke can be made about her being J. Edgar Hoover in disguise. A Chinese man can appear in a more recent film specifically as the owner of a Chinese curio shop.

But giving an African-American or an Asian a substantive role as a lawyer, doctor, policeman, teacher, etc., without calling specific attention to their ethnicity is beyond him. To clarify: In *Top Gun* Tom Cruise plays a young man. His ethnicity is unimportant, and never mentioned. In *Far and Away*, he plays a young Irishman, and his ethnicity is central to the story. In *Sea of Love*, Al Pacino plays a man. In *The Godfather*, he plays an Italian.

In other words, the roles in *Top Gun*, and *Sea of Love* could conceivably have gone to any actor, but the roles in *Godfather* and *Far and Away* could only have gone to an actor of European descent.

Far too often, when minorities appear in movies, it is as minorities. Their ethnicity looms larger than their humanity.

Why? Because this is the approach most comforting to America. If America didn't like it, such films wouldn't thrive in the marketplace.

So, in the sense that neither seems to capable of looking beyond the skin to the human being beneath, Woody Allen and Spike Lee are twin peas in the same sick pod. The difference is that Spike has had to deal with the race question virtually every day of his life, and Woody Allen has been able to hide from it. Both are enormously successful. Both give America precisely what it wants to see.

Enormous gains have been made, but the popular mythology remains elitist and separatist. It is changing, and I would expect that its media manifestations will reflect what Americans want to see, and will therefore be an accurate, unbiased measurement of the realities of race relations in America. I'm watching. Closely.

And believe it or not, optimistically.

And meanwhile, thank God, my city isn't burning.

Steven Barnes is an acclaimed Science Fiction novelist

The Myths of "Black Racism" and The Shockleytizing of America

George F. Sanders

For many whites, "Black Racism" has become an enticing device to deny their culture's bond with racism. The demagoguery of attaching "Black Racism" to blacks also tries to deny the fact that whites inherited racism. Racism, like a tar baby, clings to whites spiteful of efforts to shed its stigma as many whites still cling to it. Therefore, sole possession of racism, the idea of one race's superior right to rule over another, belongs to white people.

"Black Racism," is a racist bifurcation which tends to hunt down victims — just as escaped slaves were tracked down because they were "property," then punished because they "stole" the property — themselves. A couple of centuries later, the State of Wisconsin prosecutes a black man, not for the beating of a white youth, but because his "racist taunts" caused the beating. "Black Racism? Hardly. The ease to discard the effects of racism upon that black man is on par with the reluctance of whites to face up to racism's diabolical grip on America.

Guilt and clout, in the absence of compassion, also eases the creation of victims. Clout, or power, makes it go. Some blacks confuse success with power and credit "Black Racism" as part of some integration process by ignoring that "right to rule" is couched in power, real or imagined. Blacks have little such power and are still last in line. Power forces the parlaying of far-fetched ideas to blame victims whether there is a basis in fact or not. "Black Racism" is one such idea. The proof lies in America's history of racism, by and "for white people only" and is a charge almost too easy to make — even as whites today hold dearly to William Shockley's lie about blacks and genetics.

The roots of racism go back before 18 million white immigrants flooded the U.S. from 1840 to 1920 which included Austrians, Czechs, Danes, Irish, and Italians, Jews, Germans, Hungarians, Norwegians, Poles, Slovaks, and Swedes. Poor, jobless, purged from repressive political and religious systems, they had bare time to enjoy the fresh freedoms and nationalities which distanced them from the bitter and horrendous memories of their own hells of rot in the old country.

There was little time or money to be racist, let alone conjure up fantasies about blacks being racist for their experiences with blacks were not unlike experiences among their own — everybody trying to make it. Most blacks were still catching hell at the expense of the prosperity the poor immigrants would soon enjoy. Many of that 18 million suffered bigotry from those who owned the prosperity. Not yet would they share in the power gained through the bartering of human property by their kindred long before they herded their tattered selves across the waters to new opportunity. In less than one eighth of a generation some would join the clans of bigots and racists and a few others would participate in black lynchings.

Racism, like rape, is rooted in power derived from dehumanization. Those preceding the immigrants gained power by the heinous acts against the Indians, and subsequently, from the chattel slavery of blacks — enjoining both cultures from sharing in discovered human dignity that was not theirs to covet. They are the great, great, grand-racists of those today whose powerful bellows call for welfare and prison reform, more police and a recognition of "Black Racism."

Racism is a white practice — from the castigation of Muhammad Ali for his "vision" about the Vietnam War, to the recent refusal to seat black secret service men in a northern Denny's Restaurant, to the charges that squashed Lani Guinier's chance to head the Justice Department's civil rights division. All white. Yet, whites beg the question of "Black Racism?!!" Where? When? What did it DO!!?

Whites may demand, "What about black racist attacks on Oriental and Asian Americans who have businesses in black areas?" A few blacks may agree, but both proponents have been suckered by the suffusion of race and color, again, to veil racism and to dilute its connection to whites.

Black frustration and anger has victimized America's more recent immigrants Oriental and Asians, by illegally wrecking their businesses located in black neighborhoods and causing serious injuries and death. This is not "Black Racism." Frustrated blacks are not stupid. It first takes intelligence to become angry. But unremitted frustration short-circuits rationality. Those blacks know their run-down-dilapidated neighborhoods are products of job discrimination and segregated housing and having no choice to escape it, choose

to possess it. Any "funny attitudes," real or imagined, on their turf is bound to be dealt with. "Did you hear what the f— that sumbitch SAY?!!" "Tear this muthaf— UP!" RIP! " . . . take that!" SMASH! " . . . comin' down here!" SMASH! " . . . thinking yu gon rip off!" [. . . and I ain't got a job!] POW! [and the rent du!} KICK! STOMP! No racism here; just a boilover.

These isolated attacks are hardly any different from the LAPD cops' (who probably are not racists) beating of Rodney King, that was jump-started from the frustrating fury at possibly being killed by chasing a nut at 100 miles an hour on their violent turf. "Didya see, by Gawd, whad da fock da sonufabitch DID?!!" "Tear da bastard UP!" WHIP! " . . . take that!" WOP! " . . . ya trying ta get me offed . . . " ZAP! " . . . drivin like ya won da Indanaplis 500, huh!" KICK! [and my wife wants a damn divorce!] KICK! [. . . my kid's smoking grass!] STOMP! KICK! STOMP! STOMP! STOMP! No racism here; another boilover. Parents almost do the same thing to their children sometimes.

The majority of relationships between Oriental and Asian ethnics with businesses in black segregated neighborhoods and their customers is without confrontation or tragedy. As is with the majority arrests of speeding blacks by white cops. Both occasional tragedies may have little to do with racism and nothing to do with the fallacy, "Black Racism." Both do little to amplify racism's already built-in proliferation.

For whites to finger Blacks who beat up other minorities and whites as "Black Racists" denies the existence of environments where, but for racism, confrontations are few. Whites may want to assume that segregated neighborhoods and natural things — and, by brokering "Black Racism," search for unrealities to escort a justification for control and power — even over other whites. "Black Racism," and its twin, "reverse discrimination," which discounts its forward mode, together skew civil rights by favoring legislation that mocks democracy, but wins the sentiment of white bigots.

Yet, there is more to this. The phrase, "Black Racism" tends to muddy the identities of racist and racism, thereby diverting attention elsewhere. Another white thing. It does not mean all whites are racists. However, it does suggest that racism is not just centered among the Neo-Nazis who want to ship blacks back to Africa. Given the climate of segregated America, more than a few fed-up Blacks might take this group at its word were there a free one-way, no-catch, trip in the offering.

Should such an idea blossom, conceivably an unusual haste in government would squelch a mass black exodus to halt the inevitable bloodshed by those same Nazis as their pure-white illusion of tranquility vanishes upon seeing themselves becoming America's new niggers.

Neither all government or big business is racist, yet they represent the primary culprits. In 1989, white contractors, in Richmond, VA., claimed that a 30% minority setaside program was "reverse-discrimination" and "endangered their jobs." The Supreme Court supported the contention, and in lock step local municipalities across the country stopped similar programs which destroyed hundreds of minority businesses. Lately, white scientist, as if to punctuate the Court's ruling have jumped into the fray Shockley fashion — to trivialize the recriminations against blacks and open the door extended labeling, like "Black Racism."

Nevertheless, We Americans tend to colloquialize anything and "Black Racism" is no different. Some

white folks think that if a black person hates them, is snobbish to other blacks, and wants nothing to do with either and says so, he or she is a "Black Racist." This may be bigotry, but not racism. Understanding the distinctions between the two requires recognizing power and how little power blacks have in affecting values even within their own segregated cultures. Some whites may be upset by uppity blacks who believe themselves superior, or whose spouse having some kind of right to rule. Well, they don't rule and have no sustainable power to discriminate or segregate.

Various groups might diminish others by anything they can get their hands on — religion, ethnicity, sexual preference, short people, etc., etc., yet it takes power to nurture, fan and sustain the levels of discrimination and segregation of people based upon the color, black. This is racism and it is endemic among *all* whites.

One may sympathize with the victimization of white females and white homosexuals. Yet, their burden hardly matches that heaped upon blacks for they, being white, maintain proximities to the rich and powerful that few blacks possess. By patterning their beat after the '60's civil rights marches, singing, sit-ins, and head-get-beat-ins by blacks, white females have netted more in a couple of years (with gays bringing up the rear) than blacks have in two hundred. Both groups now claim to be minorities — a grandiose idea having given rise to the aberrations, "female sexism" and "gay homophobia" which are just as silly as "Black Racism."

The absurdity of "Black Racism," is nurtured by those who may or may not be racists. They include blacks, author Shelby Steel, Supreme Court Justice Clarence Thomas, columnist Clarence Page of the Chicago Tribune, and Juan Williams of the

Washington Post; and, white writers, William Buckley, Mike Royko, and George Will. By avoiding and/or attacking the politics of quotas, affirmative action and setasides, they create public "comfort-zones" which allow racist ideas to flourish.

This group negates the holocaust of 30 million blacks during the 17th and 18th century slave years plus 20th century efforts of blacks and whites who picketed and were beaten trying to change America's look at people of color. Steel, Thomas, Page and Williams all benefitted from having either lucky or frugal fore-parents, or from just plain hard work. All four shy from affirmative action and setaside talk and go into overdrive at the scant mention of the dreaded quotas. Steel champions that all blacks have to do is get off their butts. Thomas will for long have nightmares about the racist national main event centered around his confirmation. Page deftly straddles both sides of the isle to keep his T.V. ratings intact. Williams has complicated his successes by allegedly getting socked with on-the-job sexual harassment charges.

None of four are "Black Racists" for they have little real power and their critical actions reflect only that within the context of white racism. However, the influential scores of Buckley, Royko and Will have been nursemaided with strong stuff . . . a few hundred years of racism. All three have made pro-references to

"Black Racism" and represent the vanguard in legitimizing the term.

Yet, the above group combined are two-bit pokers compared to the impact of transistor expert, William Shockley, Ph.D, and his nation-shaking 1970's research on black genetics. Was Shockley, who was white and probably not racist, paid by racist to do it? Were they "Black Racist?" Most likely not, yet blacks failed to effectively expose who and why, and too late, tried damage control on the professor's racist "findings." This is a lack of power.

Scattered challenges and outstanding rebuttals by black professor Mary Berry finally revealed Shockley's flawed data. However, the racist ideas became hot white news, branded on the backsides of the white public, singed in the psyches of white powerbrokers, and which today still Shockleytize white America about black citizens having genetic disposition for low intelligence, welfare and crime. This is power; this is racism and it is unrivaled among whites.

Long-term segregated environments deny blacks options that are readily available to others. A recent study "Hypersegregation in U.S. Metropolitan Areas: Black and Hispanic Segregation Along Five Dimensions" suggests that racism and segregation "isolates a minority group from amenities, opportunities and resources that affect social and economic well-being," and "understates the severity of segregation." (Douglas Massey and Nancy Denton, University of Chicago, 1989) Massey's study underscores the fact that even middle-class blacks have a hard time escaping segregation's economic stigma. Those who succeed fail to shed racism's deadly psychological effects. This impacts upon the values within black segregated communities as it did on plantations. In-tra-cultural biases overlap economic classes such as that between light-skinned and dark-skinned blacks, between blacks with "good" straight-haired, thin lipped, narrow-nosed caucasian features vs. "bad" nappy haired, large-lipped, flat nosed Negroid features.

The prejudices in and among the black culture are echoed of extended and sustained racism, discrimination and segregation. The phrase, "If you are white, you alright; if you brown, stick around; if you black, get back," has resurfaced in many all-black environments. This is repression, not "Black Racism."

Early generation blacks pinched their children's noses and succumbed to black entrepreneur Madame Walker's Skin whitener ads by plastering the sticky white cream on their faces to become lighter. Powerful turn-white technology was not available as that used by Michael Jackson and designed to assure that no white Elvis-types would try to rip-off his crotch-grabbing routines. This is about as close to "Black Racism" as one will get, but Michael is now white (?), so maybe not.

Black people, generally, have no capacity to escape the segregated entrapments called neighborhoods and communities. The powers of systematic and institutional racism still discriminate against blacks in equal opportunity for jobs and contracts. Racism offers segregated public schools the choice of paltry, inadequate budgets or privatization by greedy white corporations about to hustle black kids. Worse, racism conditions consequences similar to 14th century feudal or 17th century colonial sub-cultures — of self-destruction, violence and competition between black men, and black men and black women "for master's favor."

Black women are more hip to what goes on here. Too many black men settle for mimicking sexist white males and who manage top-feeder levels in segregated urban "poverty tanks" administered by white suburbanites. Black women and their families become subject to the perfunctory designs that keep things as they are, because they are lowest on the power scale.

The feudal/colonial systems, based on the raw powers of a few over a powerless many, dissipated either by revolutions or the renascences coming by chattel slavery. What will it take to change the new high-tech poor, black sub-cultures captured in what are called "communities?"

Whites are not born racists. Why is it so easy to learn? What happens to racism when both blacks and whites are in combat. What happens socially to the integrated Phoenix Suns' players after game-time? Is that important? How does one separate bias or prejudice from racism? Does simple observation of its practice provide clues to its casual properties? Must blacks fight racism with racism without power to do so. When they gain the power to do it, is it right? Is power what it is all about? A good look at the present world may provide some answers.

International markets tolerate neither incompetence nor its precursor, inefficiency — nor, big being best as forty-year-ago third-raters, Germany and Japan push America's face into second place. White America can no longer afford to allow only its white "good old boys" to make decisions on everything, all the time, about everybody, everywhere, then blame its costly boo-boos (Vietnam, Agent Orange, toxic waste, pollution, spotted owl, trade deficit, the national debt) on others who were excluded from participating in those decisions.

This is racism and its white side effects, discrimination and segregation, which void the efficiencies of better that 20% of the country's people — Blacks, Hispanics, Indians, etc, who readily fight the country's wars, then return to the same degradation they left.

Racism is a disease like alcoholism. People of color — mostly immune to its contagion, other white people — must quit reacting only to its prognosis and develop their own alternate regimens for the prevention of racism's havoc. Whites, willing to cooperate, may help. Calling the "pot black," will not help. Fishing for super-scapegoats like, "Black Racism" won't either.

For this to continue permits whites to be comfortable in using blacks as footstools — excluding them from decision-making and dreams. Until blacks cease scattering powerless responses and use part of the leverage most don't realize they have to target racism and all that it represents for dissection, whites will persists in coining shortcuts to their own short-comings like "reverse discrimination" and "Black Racism;" and, other transparent mollifications to take themselves, white people themselves, off the hook.

George Sanders is a graphic artist. His writings have been published in the Milwaukee Journal and The New York Daily News.

Currently, he is starting his own publication, The PROFESSIONALS, . . . the sweeter the juice which will feature creative unusual new twists about up and coming blacks.

The Many Shades of BLACKNESS

Richard G. Carter

"If you're white, you're alight. If you're brown, stick around. But if you're black, get back..."
—Anon

Black-on-black color prejudice, like black-on-black crime, always has been part and parcel of the black experience in this country. And despite a thinly veiled veneer of racial togetherness wrought by a seemingly pro-black White House, 1993 is no exception.

Among African-Americans, light-skin is once again in, and dark skin is on the way *out* — if not already there. Make no mistake about it, those with lighter skin often feel superior to their darker brothers and sisters.

The reasons are relatively simple, but may be difficult for some — especially holier-than-thou, ultra-liberal whites — to accept. Moreover, many blacks may not like to hear the reasons and some may not accept them. But who said truth-telling was acceptable?

To begin with, *every* American over 40 — regardless of race —knows that white folks have it much easier than black folks in the land of the free and the home of the brave. I challenge any white person who disputes this to walk in my shoes for a day and see how you like it.

You wouldn't. I guarantee it.

That's because not a single 24-hour period goes by that somehow, somewhere, I am not reminded of my race and color — by word, gesture or deed — in some subtle or overt way. I kid you not.

This can happen in a supermarket, elevator, restaurant, doctor's office, bank, subway, commuter train, airplane, reading the paper, watching TV, driving a car, at a ball game, talking to a cop, in court, on a date, in the backyard or at work — regardless of job, financial condition or status in life.

The reminder *usually* is a white person or institution — but not always. For example, whites aren't as likely to outwardly call us nigger these days, but many black folks have no such compunction. Although often in jest — but not always — this particular racial epithet uttered by blacks nonetheless reminds us of who, and what, we are and always have been, in America.

The latter is a manifestation of self-hate gleaned from generations of being forced to accept white standards of everything from soup to nuts — including physical appearance.

Therefore, it stands to reason that blacks who resemble whites in skin tone (and, to a large degree, in the texture of their hair) are able to make their way with less hassle. That's because, like it or not, most people feel more comfortable among those who look like them — *especially* the white majority in this country.

Thus, over the years, some light-skinned blacks have embraced the advantages of being white (or close to it) by willingly "passing." Some are never found out. Others "pass" only when it suits them, like a light-skinned, wavy-haired cousin of mine.

Some of the latter are "outed" in embarrassing fashion, as was my cousin, on several occasions. But he continued to "pass" during his travels in the late 1950s and throughout the '60s when many hotels were segregated. He also found it useful in dating white women.

Spike Lee's dazzling 1988 movie *School Daze*, put the color problem among blacks in disturbing, albeit humorous perspective. In the film, a group of light-skinned students at an all-black college were dubbed "wannabees" (as in "want to be less black and more white") and their dark-skinned counterparts who had a sense of racial identity were called "jigaboos."

The wannabees, of course, "acted" and "dressed" white and the jigaboos, did the opposite. Although audience laughter flowed freely, the underlying theme of internecine color prejudice among African-Americans was brought kicking and screaming to the surface.

Tragically, this color caste system occasionally erupts into verbal and even physical confrontations.

Some darker-skinned young blacks have been known to react violently after enduring the taunts of those with lighter skins, while others have simply sought to vent their color-based frustrations by seeking out and abusing those who used to be referred as "high yellows."

I vividly recall an ugly public incident one evening a few years ago in a crowd outside a movie house in a large midwestern city. After the feature ended a half-dozen or so "brown-skin" black youths began to heckle two very dark African college students in their early 20s who were with two nice looking young light-skinned women.

"That nigger's so black till he's blue," was one of the particularly memorable comments made. The targets of the tastelessness began to heckle back, and only the determined intervention of the females — also students — prevented a full-scale brawl.

While retaliation is somewhat understandable, premeditated verbal and physical abuse is *not*. Yet, as in the days when me and some of my unenlightened early-teen friends used to go "honkey-hunting" — looking for defenseless white kids to beat up — it does happen. I remember at least a half-dozen occasions when I've witnessed color-based name-calling initiated by dark-skinned black teenagers. The epithets, usually aimed at wavy-haired very light blacks, ranged from "pale face" to "yellow-jello" to "pink eyes" to "white boy."

But adults are not immune. Like the time a dark-skinned waiter in his early 60s refused to serve two light-skinned black couples seated near my wife and I in a predominantly white restaurant. We wondered why, and on our way out I asked the waiter.

"No class," he whispered to me. "I can always tell by the way they look at me. You know, the kind of white-black folks who wouldn't go to a black doctor or lawyer or admit they watch *Sanford and Son* on TV."

This is just some of what the color of our skins has done to the collective psyches of African-Americans.

However, there are many "white-looking" blacks who do everything in their power to proclaim their innate blackness. The latter is perfectly personified by light-skinned, 41-year-old Benita Porter, ex-model and author of *Colorstruck*, a novel which examines the white-looking phenomena against the backdrop of black show business.

Porter, a resident of the New York City suburb of Mount Vernon, grew up in Columbus, Ohio, where she quickly felt the racist barbs of whites *and* blacks who refused to believe she could belong to her light-skinned, though clearly black mother.

"People would openly ask my mother, 'Is this your child?' Porter said. "And to this day, people ask me, 'What are you?'"

On the other hand, Porter said, her father "who was very much a reverse racist, was light and mistaken for white all the time. And he'd lecture the family at the dinner table every night in the '50s, '60s and '70s on America's racial problems."

The statuesque Porter said she adopted much of her father's militancy at Tennessee State University, where she wore the biggest Afro hairstyle on campus in tribute to her idol, light-skinned black activist Angela Davis. She also wore dashiki tops and dresses — aimed at trying to fit in and identify with black people.

These days, however, many light-skinned blacks seem more interested in becoming acceptable to the white majority than in touting their African roots. By so doing, they feel, they stand a better chance of getting better jobs and living in better neighborhoods.

While there certainly is nothing wrong with attempting to better one's self, doing so by putting down their dark-complexioned, nappy-haired fellow blacks through lack of association and a superior attitude is like barking up the wrong tree.

Doing so by buying into the white-yuppie get ahead at all costs dog shit that marked the 1980s under the out-of-touch Ronald Reagan and George Bush and continue unabated under Billy (Liar) Clinton, is the pits. To do *this*, of course, means you need someone to look down upon. For light-skinned blacks, it's their dark-skinned brethren.

Finally, the many unfortunate African-Americans who feel light skin, thin lips, narrow noses and wavy-to-straight hair gives them an edge over their opposite numbers in the black community should have been with me in a Black Muslim mosque in 1965 to hear Cassius Clay shortly after his conversion to Islam. Said the new Muhammad Ali:

"Rich black earth is best. Strong black coffee is best. The judge wears a black robe and you call him 'Your honor.' The blacker the berry the sweeter the juice. . . "

The lesson being: Most black folks regardless of color are simply that — blacks — to most white folks. Besides, who's to say who's the richest or better looking, Michael Jackson or Michael Jordan. Uh-huh.

The Necessary Racist

Craig Thompson

I am the necessary racist. If I didn't exist, I'd have to.

I became aware of race at age five, one hot summer day. My father took a wrong turn in Baltimore on the way to the airport to pick up my grandmother. At a stop sign, in a neighborhood of rundown brownstones, three black boys saw us and, finding stones, pelted our blue Buick. "Why are those boys throwing rocks?" I asked my parents in the front seat, their silence overcome by the whine of a speeding engine.

Such was my introduction to the American dilemma. Years later, into my teens on the other side of the continent, on an equally hot summer day, I listened to a young black woman wearing a black beret. I'd volunteered to work with black kids at a school in South Park, a neighborhood bordered by the city limits so the town's business leaders could boast there was no slum in Santa Rosa. Dick Gregory and Martin Luther King inspired me to join the civil rights movement as I could in my community. The young woman, up from Oakland with a couple of other Panthers for escort, also inspired.

"If any of these white people," she said, "give you any shit, you give it back double. And don't let any of them tell you you're wrong, cause you are not wrong, they are wrong, they are all racists." Silence fell among us, a glass curtain. In the eight weeks I spent organizing community events in South Park, we never saw the Panthers again.

I had not yet become my future. College came, Whitworth, up in Spokane, where Jim Minor and I befriended each other, brothers under skin. Jim dark, rich from the Lower Eastside in all ways but money, me debatably redhead, sophomoric, poor. Our friendship lasted longer than our girl friends, till the summer after Jim graduated. We moved in with another black guy, whose basement bedroom was next to mine. One morning I woke to hear my neighbor beating up a woman. Later, another woman I knew told me the same guy had held a derringer to her head, forcing her to perform oral sex on him. Jim didn't know how this guy behaved, and I didn't know how to tell him. I moved into a dorm, and Jim wondered why I'd left so quickly; I never explained, even when he relocated to the coast for a job. The glass wall I'd first known on a hot California day had entered our friendship.

I did not know then I was the necessary racist. I counted people of color as friends, partied and lived with them, applying history's hard lessons to myself. By the late 70's, new masters degree in hand, I went to teach GIs in West Germany. I intended to bring academic skills of soldiers up to the demands of military training. The Basic Skills Education Program taught me that after 30 years of integration, racial distrust was common in the army. My classes were a third black, a third Hispanic, a third white, groups keeping mostly to themselves. One black GI confided after a training exercise, "Out there we play at war, but the real war is in the barracks, and it's a race war."

Tension broke out on base between Americans or off base with xenophobic Germans. One afternoon in class, as I walked by a big black GI named Peters, I heard a fist slam on the table. I turned to see Peters' honest, frustrated face. "Tommy," he said, giving me another name, "it ain't you." I believed him then; I still do.

Back in the states, I accepted a teaching position at The Evergreen State College, a place noted for its progressive reputation. For over three years, I worked as a writing instructor in a facility called the Learning Resource Center, or LRC, teaching rhetoric, grammar, literature, and creative writing to a broad range of students. It was at Evergreen I fulfilled my destiny as the necessary racist.

In the Fall quarter, 1983, one of my students agreed to work with a young woman named Davina, the head of Evergreen's black student union, to sponsor a reading by two important black women writers in the Northwest. For three quarters, Davina misled first one of my students and then another, but I didn't pursue the issue with her until, in spring 1984, I walked into her office and calmly asked if she was going to help with the reading, two weeks away. In the room were three witnesses to my words; the same three heard Davina's.

"This white boy has given me shit all year! I've had enough of your shit! Don't you know how important a poet I am?" She continued yelling at me, drawing people from other offices. For five minutes I stood, stunned while she hurled racial epithets and boasted of a fame she did not possess. I stepped out to a familiar silence, shaking my head at the small crowd. Davina followed me to my office and apologized, promising she'd cook dinner for the visiting writers, design and distribute posters, and take care of all publicity.

She did none of these. She did talk a friend of hers, who hadn't witnessed our scene, into complaining about me with her to the Director of the Educational Support Programs, a strong black man who called himself Stone whose responsibilities included overseeing the center where I worked and the Third-World student groups. He set a date for a meeting to discuss Third-World views of the Learning Resource Center and closed his door to me until then.

I went about my instructional duties. As news travels fast in a small college, my Third-World students knew the hand I'd been dealt but they didn't know what to do. Nor did I. I trusted Stone would do what was right, even though he once called my Norwegian ancestors, "The worst of the Europeans." I knew him to be proud, but I believed him to be fair. I was half right.

The Tuesday of our meeting, I arrived on campus, not suspecting what would happen that afternoon. I went into the cafeteria to buy a cup of coffee and walked over to the building where I worked. Half an hour later, I learned an obsessed male student had murdered his former girl friend in the cafeteria minutes after I left, killing her with a .45 automatic pistol. A large number of my students either witnessed the killing or knew the couple involved. I spent most of my morning with people who needed to talk about the murder that had touched them. By the time my one o'clock meeting arrived, I was already in shock from the events of the morning. By three o'clock I was in greater shock, not only from the killing, but from what I had become.

Three others attended: Stone; my immediate supervisor in the center, Stella, a handicapped, conservative Christian in her late 50s; and a Japanese American woman who called herself "Hisami," though this was not her real name. Hisami had worked in the LRC and in student groups, considering herself a spokesperson for all Third-World people on

campus, though no Third-World students I knew considered her such. I was surprised to see her, as she wasn't present the day Davina and I met. I did expect to see Davina, but Stone explained though she and her friend were invited, they decided not to attend. I never had opportunity to meet my accusers and answer their accusations. To Stone, this was apparently all right.

The meeting was turned over to Hisami. For 15 minutes, she commented on how I would tell people their spelling or grammar was wrong. This was a lie; my teaching technique was always to show people how to be more effective in writing, not to label their work. Why she lied was obvious. Hisami was fond of explaining, "Only white people can be racist, because the -ist word ending means someone who believes in a system, and the only system we have is a white-controlled system, so only white people can be racist." She learned this in a course called "Third-World Wisdom," and repeated it in my presence on a number of occasions to student aides in the center, relishing power over naive young white people. The reason she wanted to attend this particular meeting was clear. It gave her a chance to be racist without being called on it.

When she left, I expected my supervisors and I would have a professional discussion. I was wrong. "Now you shut up," Stone said, thrusting a finger in my face, "and just listen." For over an hour, they took turns berating me.

At first, I didn't understand why Stella acted the way she did, but over the next 40 days, I learned she was paranoid the administration would close our center if they learned half our students were third- and fourth-year students whose full-time professors hadn't taught them anything about writing.

I was told I was to have a year's unpaid leave of absence. On my last day on the job Stella said, "Everybody thinks you're coming back but you don't have a job here anymore because you're just after my job." I told her I didn't want her job; I just wanted my own. Stella, for all her fear about the school's administration, was merely an accessory. It was Stone who made me the necessary racist.

In the last six weeks I taught at Evergreen, I approached Stone several times. I told him I'd been misrepresented; he told me to leave. He never contacted any of the witnesses who saw Davina's conduct that day. The truth of what actually happened was not important; what was important was a racially based opinion Stone could not or would not disown. Wasn't I an uppity white boy? Didn't a young black woman accuse me of disrespect?

I had become the necessary racist, a creation of other people's minds. It did not matter that every Third-World student I'd taught at the college praised my teaching. It did not matter that, during my years there, I brought more Hispanic, Native American, and African American writers to the college than the rest of the faculty combined. It did not matter that I developed curriculum to include Third-World and feminist perspectives not because it was politically correct, but because the writing was good. It did not matter that I'd spent much of my life advocating human and civil rights. All that mattered to Stone, Hisami, Davina, and the other petty bigots at Evergreen was the color of my skin. I was the necessary racist, essential to their prejudice.

The night of the reading, Davina bumped into me and promised she'd see me there. She didn't show up. Her friend who had complained to Stone about me did, arriving half way through, avoiding my eyes when I greeted her. The writers had a small audience, not suspecting the controversy behind their appearance, words reflecting their personal struggles. Mine was ongoing. Later, when I walked into the cabin I rented, my phone was ringing It was Davina. "I'm sorry," she said, her words marking me forever. "You took a fall for my anger." I said it was over; it wasn't.

My relationship with my immediate supervisor went to hell, each day her demands becoming more irrational. Stella told me I was responsible for reminding her about meetings I didn't know she had. She made me accountable for writing evaluations of students who were not my responsibility. She went out of her way on a daily basis to find fault with anything I did or said, even sending a condescending letter to my home and phoning to harass me after work.

Towards the end, I said I'd had enough and went to the Director of Personnel about the harassment. I met with her, a large black woman who promised to intervene on three occasions; her word was worthless. I suspected Stone had her ear, their offices near each other, my reputation preceding me through his interpretation. Later, she would deny me reimbursement of accumulated leave, allowing Stone to decide that surgery to remove four impacted wisdom teeth during my last week of insurance coverage didn't count as sick leave. It was the last insult to injury Stone could contrive. With this blatant dishonesty, he and The Evergreen State College violated state law, a violation documentable, verifiable.

I talked to lawyers and got three opinions. All agreed my rights had been violated, while agents of the college had committed fraud in lying to me about my year's leave of absence that was never a leave of absence. I could prove I was railroaded, buffaloed by bigots, my teaching career permanently damaged by people I trusted who were not trustworthy. Finally, I decided to let it go. Rebuilding my life was more important than destroying the careers of those who lacked the personal courage to face up to what they had done, or their shallow reasons why.

I taught for a few years in the community colleges, hoping for full-time work that never materialized, finding them as full of stupid politics as Evergreen. I kept working on human rights issues, particularly with Native Americans, though I pissed some AIM members off when I called them on racial remarks made at the expense of black people. Today, I live in a mixed neighborhood, as mixed as the blood I carry. My grandfather's grandfather fought the U.S. Cavalry, his ancestors followed a landbridge from Asia, while others spread north and to the east to wind up poor Norwegians sailing off to stolen land. No matter the road chosen, we all first stood on that distant African plain.

To those who say only white people can be racist, I answer your belief proves your bigotry. To those who want us in hate's stronghold, I advise doing the right thing is more than seeing a movie. I have been the racist of your past, I have known the futility of your anger, and though you may need me to be as you judge, I can only define myself by who I am, not by who you blame.

REVERSE RACISM OR SELF DEFENSE?

SEATON B. HANCOCK

So, okay . . . Perhaps you've heard this one:

"What's twelve inches and white?"

"Nothing!"

Cute, right? Yeah, I laughed, too when I first heard it. Even told some friends as we sat around telling our favorite one-liners. Mind you, though, considering I'm black and they're white, it's kind of weird telling a joke that says, "Hey, you guys are hung like hamsters!" I mean, no offense, it's only a joke, right? Besides, *I'm* still wondering who started the one about my brethren being hung like telephone poles . . . Anyway, one friend of mine innocently asked me why recently there's been a rash of black comedians taking on whitey with no holds barred.

"Self defense," I told her.

I thought about what I said, and well, it *is* true to an extent. I mean, often we blacks resort to humor when we find ourselves without any other outlet to vent our spleen. I mean, there's always rap, which often removes the kid gloves and goes for the jugular. [By the way, I find it oddly humorous to see a white kid with a Public Enemy T-shirt. I mean, dig, rap groups are often branded as anti-white . . . Oh excuse me, "We're not anti-white, we're only pro-black." (Yeah, right on.)]

I'm not necessarily angry, but, well, when I mentioned the white kid with the Public Enemy T-shirt, I think

of other phenomena of related instance (Hey — pretty hifalutin' language for one of a race not associated with "proper" vocabulary, huh?) . . . Anyway . . . I've noticed that throughout the decades, Black Culture has been assimilated into and patronized by White Culture. I mean, dig this list:

Remember Vanilla Ice? (Go ahead, try!)

How 'bout the Blues Brothers? (Their movie superiority was *stolen* by it's "guest stars," such as Aretha Franklin, Ray Charles, Cab Callaway, and the mighty James Brown.)

How about *American Bandstand*? (My family used to tune in and *laugh* before switching to *Soul Train*.)

Oh, hey, what about the Rolling Stones? ("Brown sugar! How do you taste so good? Brown sugar! Just like a black girl should!") Dig, it's also a known *fact* that black acts have opened for them throughout the years . . . Just ask Ike & Tina Turner, Prince, or Living Color.

Eric Clapton can cover "I Shot the Sheriff" but Ice-T can't rap about cop-killers!

Oh — Anybody remember Wild Cherry? "PLAY THAT FUNKY MUSIC, *WHITE BOY*!!!"

Hell, the President himself was seen on tee-vee with dark glasses honking into a saxophone!!!! (Goin' for the cool vote, huh, Prez?)

I mean, whew!, I *could* go on, y'know . . . but I'm only saying that, well, I wonder . . . Are you complimenting us or ripping us off? Are you asking for soul by proxy or merely saying "Huh!! You ain't special, we can do it, too!" (Yeah, right, white men *can* jump; just ask Larry Bird!) I mean, some of you even damn your own pale skin and go all out for tanning, which as we all know promotes sunburn, wrinkling, heatstrokes, and skin cancer!!

Anyway, with all this going on, we as a race are still held at arms length. You dig our music, our fashions, and our "hip talk," but we still get beaten up on nationwide TV (literally and stereotypically!). So, *naturally* rappers and comedians are gonna Dis your white ass!! It's easy, too. I mean, as troublesome a race as we are claimed to be, we don't have sickos like Jim Jones, Jeffrey Dahmer, Charles Manson, and that dude in

Waco in our camp. It would SURELY be in the news if we did!

Oh, before you brand me as "uppity," please consider this: I don't condone racism, regardless of where it comes from. I'm only saying that the ammunition is readily available. Los Angeles should not have gone up in flames, but, mind you, it was rage and frustration strained to the breaking point. I don't condone rappers' comments on Jews and Koreans, but if you've been an underdog for so long you'd wanna blame somebody, too, right? I mean, if you've been constantly under scrutinization, patronization, ridicule, hate, and outright violence, wouldn't *you* be a little "prickly?" Go ahead, just *ask* us why we often have our guard up before you even so much as *blink* at us!! Even when you extend a hand in friendship, it's often met with suspicion. Too bad, too, considering that I feel that some of y'all are on our side. I know this personally: My own ex-wife is Italian, we have a daughter, and, hey, we still get along . . . and no, we did NOT split up because of our races. In fact, to get even *further* into it, we broke up under the pressure this country places on folks, white or black, to earn a decent living and be somebody. I collapsed under pressure, and I found myself quite literally slowly going mad under the strain. I don't entirely blame her for ending the marriage — she couldn't take care of a daughter AND a progressively dysfunctional adult. (Hey, *that* happens to the best of us, y'know? Just ask Woody & Mia.)

Anyway, I'm digressing here . . .

Scooter
(the mixed-up white boy)

"...um, er, I suppose my attempt at solidarity is, um, unsatisfactory?..."

Dig, I got this pal... He's Jewish, okay? He teaches at Yeshiva University and out of respect, he wears a yarmulke in class. Once outside, he removes it. Sometimes he forgets, and he's told me of the icy stares he gets while he's wearing the damn thing. It's a shame, huh? Speaking of Jews, that incident in Crown Heights, y'know, when that driver hit and killed that kid, well, had cooler heads prevailed, it would only have been called a tragic incident. Instead, because the driver was Jewish and the child was Black, it caused an ever-widening gap between the races, accompanied by the usual racial slurs and rock-throwing. Pity, y'know? I mean, considering that Jews & Blacks have historically been doormats for much of Western Civilization, I've always felt that they should unite and kick some SERIOUS ass!!!

Yo, *I've* been dissed by my own "homies" for *hanging out* with you guys!

"When the revolution comes down, who's side *you* gonna be on?"

"Why don't you go back down to Greenwich Village with your white friends and leave us the fuck alone?"

I mean, like, ouch, y'know? ...

I was playing music in Washington Square park with this brother — I play sax and he was playing guitar — and this photographer, who was white, snapped our picture. The brother took offense and wanted to bust his head!! During the resulting altercation, we were surrounded by a group of black youths who didn't even *KNOW* what the shit was about and wanted to kick the photographer's ass. I asked why; I mean, he was only snapping our picture. I was called "Uncle Tom" and was chased out of the park!

Oy *vey*, Muthafucka!!

Anyway, you might understand what I'm getting at. In an age of stereotypes (old and new), quotas (just filled with liberal guilt & confusion), police brutality (yes, even now), and all that utterly useless racial bullshit that threatens to kill us *ALL*, I can only say, "enough, already!" I mean, *Rodney King*, f'r cryin' out loud, said, "Can't we all get along?" Sadly, though, it won't be easy. First of all, some of us out there are just gonna have to get off our high horse, y'know? I mean, we must realize that racism has gone on so long and has gone so deep that it's hard to pull it out. Some of us don't want to. It's all we know. It's all we wanna believe in. It's a sickness, a "jones," a crippling disease, and we've all gotten way too comfortable living with it. We even pass it down to our kids. God help them.

Race still continues to be an issue because we *MAKE* it so.

Dig, if one is truly secure within one's own core, one has no *need* to feel false superiority over others. Ignorance, suspicion, fear and hate need not be. We're all the same as far as humanity goes; we bleed the same blood, etcetera. In fact, we are *not* "separate *but* equal," we are DIFFERENT *AND* EQUAL. Please note the distinction I've made; it might just be the key to the puzzle.

So, check it out y'all: To my European friends out there, please allow us space, or it may be taken. To my African brothers, I can dig "By any means necessary," but only as long as the last resort isn't the first and only choice.

Peace, y'all... *everybody*.

Seaton B. Hancock (a.k.a "Chuck" Hancock a.k.a. "Raven") is a horribly gifted (and confused) renaissance man. Once a saxophonist for Joey Miserable & the Worms and Murphy's Law, now he says, "Hey, I can draw, too!!!"

BLACK RACISM: WHAT GOES AROUND COMES AROUND

Richard G. Carter

"Eeeny, meeny, miny, moe. Catch a nig. . ."

Watch out, now. Don't you say it. Although it may sound funny, this is 1993, remember?

Any yet, many of us who grew up in the '50s and '60s hearing the "Big N" uttered by whites in polite and not so polite conversation, find it ironic that so much attention is being paid these days to "Black racism." Ironic in that black people are derided for doing and saying some of the same things white people did and said when public anti-black epithets and acts were common in everything from street talk, shop talk and cocktail party talk to employment discrimination, housing discrimination and Hollywood movies.

And, of course, little has changed.

The fact that African-Americans have had to endure the slings and arrows of outrageous racism for so long, comes close, in my view, to making a case for retaliation in kind. To put it another way, it's tough to continue turning the other cheek, ala Jackie Robinson.

Does this mean I am advocating reverse bigotry? Absolutely not. I am simply saying that I can understand — and even excuse — some of what is labeled "black racism." What goes around, comes around.

For example, one of the things that sticks in my mind from my youth is the dialogue in Stanley Kramer's 1949 breakthrough film *Home of the Brave*. I can still see and hear character actor Steve Brodie, as a redneck white soldier, chortling: "Great cooks, the colored. Great singers and dancers, too. . ."

Later, he goes on to describe — in thick dialect — a black janitor in civilian life who used to say: "Boss, I ain't lazy. I'ze jest tired. I guess I was born tired. . ."

I recall slumping down in my seat much the same as I'd done in grade school when the teacher would ask us to read humiliating passages from "L'il Black Sambo," or ask the class to engage in a singalong of "Ole Black Joe."

Years later, during my own military service, I was at Camp A.P. Hill, Virginia, where my platoon of officer trainees was undergoing a week of special weapons familiarization and field problems. The commanding officer was a short, very dark-skinned Black captain with a high-pitched voice, who came to be known among the predominantly white personnel as "Captain Midnight."

One night, as a sergeant of the training cadre was explaining the next day's activities to the 40 or so second lieutenants in his charge, he mentioned the captain by his nickname. Then he grinned as he craned his neck and said: "I hope there ain't no other midnights in here."

There were the usual titters in the crowd and a few who knew me looked my way — one or two shaking their heads in embarrassment.

A few minutes later, the sergeant finished and began making his way out the barracks door. I intercepted him and, as his face turned crimson, asked him to accompany me outside into the darkness of the Company street.

The sergeant was a veteran of nearly 20 years in service and old enough to be my father, yet he stood before me at trembling attention and pleaded for my understanding and forgiveness.

He hadn't meant to be mean, he said, only funny. He was not a racist, he said, because he had many black buddies. And he certainly would not have called the CO "Captain Midnight" or asked about other "midnights" if he'd known I was in the group, he said.

Finally, he told me I could ruin his career were I to report his remarks to a higher authority. And he begged me not to take this action.

So, like a cop who lets you off the hook with a warning when you commit a minor traffic no-no, I chewed-out the sergeant and sent

him on his way — admonishing him never to do it again.

In more recent years, any number of racially inspired public insults coming my way were even more humiliating. One Saturday afternoon, while casually dressed, I was followed around by a white security guard in a suburban discount drugstore and accused in a very loud voice of shoplifting. In the confrontation that followed, my wife, who happens to be white, almost reduced the man to tears in the presence of the store manager and a couple dozen onlookers.

Particularly galling was my experience at the world-famous Explorer's Club, on the posh upper east side of New York City. Dinner was over and it was time for dessert and coffee

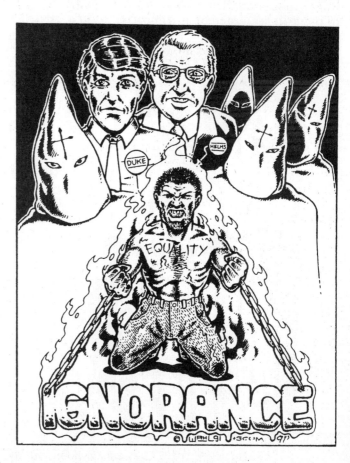

prior to a lecture by an executive at my firm who'd just returned form the South Pole. Then it happened: I was mistaken for a servant by a white male guest and asked to fetch him a cup of coffee.

Needless to say, I told the man who, like me, was wearing a dark blue suit, where he could go for his coffee. And I unceremoniously reminded him not to let the door hit him in the ass on the way out.

The point is this: As long as I can remember, there has not been a single 24 hours that passes during which I am not reminded, in some way, that I am a black person in a white world. It can be an outward and ugly comment, some noticeable form of body language or a mere wink or a glance. It can be on an elevator, a commuter train, in a supermarket checkout line, or trying to get waited on in a depart-ment store or to get seated in a nice restaurant.

If I choose to retaliate by speaking my mind about racial injustice, as does a Spike Lee or a Rev. Al Sharpton, does this make me a "black racist"? I think not. As far as I'm concerned, that's just standing up, the same as any man — white or black — should do when he is put down.

Racism — regardless of color — is never proper. It hurts too much, like sticks and stones. But if ever anyone had the right to consider talking the talk and walking the walk, it has to be African-Americans, for what we continue to endure.

Richard G. Carter, former columnist for the New York Daily News, *is a freelance writer.*

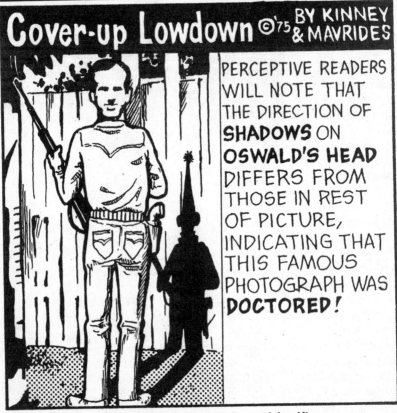

Copyright © 1977 by Paul Mavrides and Jay Kinney

VOTERS FERRETING OUT THE RIGHT STUFF

Connie Langland

Mildred Simmers of Bucktown, Chester County, is not bashful about it. She votes her religious beliefs.

Next week, she says, she'll vote for a conservative Christian slate in the local school-board primary. She's written the candidates' names on the back of a worn business card she keeps in a handy place.

"These are people who are for the moral right. I'm not interested in politics; I'm interested in God and the Bible," Simmers said on a recent morning at her son's bait shop on Route 23 in northern Chester County. Outside, a small billboard quotes Scripture: "With the Lord, there is plenteous redemption (Psalms 130:7)."

"If there's enough Christian people on the school boards all around the country, their voice is going to be heard," said Simmers.

Scores of suburban school-board seats are being contested this year. The races come at a time when controversy is flaring around the region over religion and values in the schools — over matters such as self-esteem programs, *The Color Purple*, Christmas carols, sex education, multicultural curriculums and the state's outcome-based education plan.

There is no question that some conservative Christians with strong feelings on such matters are running for school office.

The question is whether there are more of those candidates than is publicly known. Decrying what they see as a well-organized national campaign to take over the public schools, critics of the religious right say many candidates in this year's elections are keeping their religious agendas secret.

"Show yourselves," the *Kennett Paper* exhorted in an editorial last week. The Kennett Square paper criticized the conservative Pennsylvania Christian Coalition for publishing a manual that instructs members who are seeking office on to keep their affiliation a secret.

The Christian Coalition, with headquarters in Erie, is affiliated with Pat Robertson's national Christian Coalition. Retired State Rep. Peter Vroon of Valley Forge is president of its board.

"We're not going to tell you what our plans are. We're not a public outfit," Vroon said. But he added: "We don't have any weird takeover plans."

Vroon denied that the Christian Coalition would play a role in Philadelphia-area elections this year.

"We're not that well organized yet in the southeast. This is a very new effort," he said.

But in Simmons' school district — Owen J. Roberts — resident Robert Zinman sees the hand of a conservative California group, the Coalition of Excellence in Education, at work.

The head of that group, the Rev. Robert Simonds, says he has helped elect several thousand school-board members in California by developing a network of evangelical congregations and anti-abortion groups. His group seeks to restore prayer in schools and teach creationism in science classes.

Last year, Simonds called Pennsylvania "a major battleground" in conservative Christians' campaign against what they see as an agnostic education establishment intent on inculcating a secular outlook.

The reason for the focus on Pennsylvania is its outcome-based education plan. Conservative critics of the original plan said it would have enshrined the teaching of liberal values, such as tolerance of homosexuality, as a goal of public education. In response to the criticism, the plan was modified to de-emphasize the teaching of values.

Zinman is convinced he has seen evidence of a coordinated evangelical attack on public schools in Owen Roberts, where three Christian conservatives were elected to the school board in 1991. Those board members have raised objections to student assistance, breakfast, health and guidance programs.

"Everything that comes up today [in Owen Roberts] has its precedence in California," said Zinman — an accusation the conservative bloc has denied.

Zinman and others have formed a group called PEERS (People for Educational Excellence in Roberts Schools) as a counterpoint to the district's conservative group, Citizens for Responsive Education. Both groups have political action committees to raise funds. A local taxpayers' group also has weighed in with a candidates' list.

Taxpayer groups — with their mantra of no-tax-hikes-no-raises-for-teachers — have made more public noise on the school scene this spring than the religious right.

Dick Frase, who heads a coalition of local taxpayer groups called ASERT, is seeking election to the North Penn school board in Montgomery County. ASERT claims more than 30,000 members.

Frase said his group had "worked with" a state group called the Coalition for Academic Excellence, which opposes the outcome-based plan and disseminates literature from Simonds' California group. But he said area taxpayer groups had no religious ties.

"Our objectives are nonpolitical, nonreligious. We have a limited calendar and a limited purpose," said Frase. He said critics were sending "an alarmist message — that every taxpayer group is a front for the religious right."

Donna Mengel, a member of the North Penn board, describes herself as "an outspoken conservative Christian" and calls the hue and cry over religious agendas "paranoia."

"I believe conservative Christians have been around forever, and many have come to the realization that the liberal educrats have taken over the system," she said. "Without a doubt, the public-school system has fallen short — from the way we spend our money to what we're teaching our children."

But there is no conspiracy, she said. "The only Christians I hear from are the people I go to church with."

Renee Hillman, who lives just outside Bethlehem, Pa., doesn't buy such disclaimers.

Hillman, who lives in the Saucon Valley district in Northampton County, is convinced that "stealth" candidates are seeking election without revealing their religious agenda. Saucon Valley residents and clergy cringed last year when a newly elected, blunt-spoken fiscal conservative wondered aloud whether the religion of a Jewish state education official had influence the state's outcome-based education plan.

Hillman has formed something called the Freedom to Learn Network, with members in 40 districts around the state. The group has compiled 10 questions for voters to ask school candidates on such topics as vouchers, prayer in schools, creationism, sex education, book banning, and self-esteem programs.

Hillman is suspicious of so-called taxpayer candidates: "Those groups get started at a grass-roots level with real concerns about spending tax-payer dollars. But when taxpayer groups begin to question specific books, courses, curricula, I have to begin questioning their motives."

Dark warnings about "stealth" candidates exasperate Colin Hanna, a conservative Republican committeeman in Chester County.

"The issue has begun to take on the character of the Salem witch trials, where they would ask someone if they are a witch, and she would say no, and they would answer, 'Well, we figured a witch would lie,'" Hanna said.

"I am unaware of any organizational effort . . . It literally is an issue that was cooked up."

Conservative candidates do have "concerns shared in common," including "some aspects of OBE," school choice and sex education, Hanna said.

In northern Chester County, Mildred Simmer's son Fred is clear about what he finds offensive in public schools.

"They've taken God and prayer out of the public schools altogether.

I believe that when you've taken God out, you're missing the whole point of life," said Simmers.

But there other views in this neck of the woods.

Some residents skeptical of the religious right still appear wistful about bringing back some sort of school prayer, which the U.S. Supreme Court banned in 1962.

One is Kathy Lahr, who lives east of the high school on Route 23. Lahr said she didn't see how "a little bit of prayer or so" could hurt. "There are so many bad things they see, hear and learn in school — that would be a good point in their lives," said Lahr.

Others want the Owen Roberts district on concentrate on moving forward. Susan Landis, who has high praise for her local schools, lost election to the school board in 1991 and is sitting out this time around.

Said Landis: "The question is: What direction is education going to take? Is it going to go forward into the 21st century, or is it going to go backward to 1950? That's some idealized past that never existed anyway, like Ozzie and Harriet."

CHALLENGING "STEALTH" CANDIDATES

Skipp Porteous

Last summer I received a call from Ohio and heard a story that's becoming all too familiar. During the last school board election a woman ran for a seat with the promise of keeping local taxes down. This popular theme assured an easy election. Shortly after becoming elected, the woman showed up one day at the school library and demanded to see a list of library books. She proceeded to mark the books that, for one reason or another, she found offensive.

Since the 1990 "San Diego Surprise," this sort of tactic has become more and more common as newly recruited and trained Religious Right candidates enter the political system in droves — hoping to implement their theocratic agenda. (In 1993, Pat Robertson's Christian Coalition conducted two-day, intensive political training seminars called "Leadership Schools" in more than 70 U.S. cities.) San Diego County, California, witnessed the first evidence of a "stealth" campaign. In that election, some 60 out of 90 Christian Right candidates won elected seats without most voters even knowing these candidates were running. They did it by organizing

100 selected churches and creating a massive Christian phone bank.

On the Sunday before the Tuesday election, voter guides were placed under the windshield wipers of cars in church parking lots. This tactic has spread like wild fire across the country.

In most areas of the country, radical Christian Right candidates — or theocrats — are unable to win elections based upon their positions and agenda. Thus, they must resort to deception to get elected. This deception is manifested in two ways. By targeting conservative Christian voters, Religious Right candidates can appeal to them for votes. Often, just by turning out a few churches, these candidates are swept into office. By and large, other than trying to reach the church members, they don't even campaign for office. Most people are unaware of their presence until it's too late. As Free Congress Foundation head Paul Weyrich likes to say, "We don't want EVERYONE to vote."

The woman from Ohio illustrates the other form of deception. "Run on issues, any issues, that will get you elected." Sometimes a Religious Right candidate voluntarily begins a campaign this way. And sometimes they are forced to run on issues because local groups and coalitions are finding out how to undercover stealth candidates — before election day. In any case, Christian Right candidates are learning to repackage themselves so they appear more mainstream than they are. Darlee Crockett, of the Mainstream Voter's Project, has labeled this development as "Son of Stealth."

> "... despite their growing numbers, the Religious Right is a minority, and always will be."

At a Christian Coalition training session in New York City, Anthony Rivera, the city's Deputy Ombudsman, told local politicos how to run for office. As most New Yorkers are liberal or moderate Democrats, Rivera endorsed the use of deception to gain votes. "The majority of our leaders are pro-abortion," he said, "so you don't go in there and say, 'I'm an advocate against abortion.' No, you say, 'I'm interested in housing or development, or sanitation.' And you keep your personal views to yourself until the Christian community is ready to rise up, and then, wow! They're gonna be devastated!"

In 1991, the Christian Coalition held its first Road to Victory political conference in Virginia Beach, Virginia. Some 800 delegates were taught how to take over their local Republican Party from the inside,

with the ultimate goal of taking the Republican National Committee. After general sessions, groups meet in rooms set aside according to state. Here they learned the nuts and bolts of each state's Republican Party apparatus.

The 1992 Road to Victory conference followed the same format and strategy. Someone attending the Pennsylvania group meeting made an interesting discovery. (Pennsylvania, by the way, represents one of the Christian Coalition's most developed states, and is watched closely from Virginia Beach.) In the room, stacks of the new Pennsylvania County Action Plan greeted the participants. The manual told members to become directly involved in the local Republican Committee so they can become insiders. However, the manual underscored the following caution: "You should never mention the name Christian Coalition in Republican circles."

With the Rev. Pat Robertson as an example, it is no wonder the Religious Right has chosen to employ a disingenuous strategy for political involvement. In 1988, when running for President, Robertson bristled when the media referred to him as a "televangelist." He insisted that if his position with the Christian Broadcasting Network [CBN] be mentioned at all, that "religious broadcaster" was the proper label. However, at an earlier time, he went to great length to explain to his CBN staff how God had called him as a "prophet," and as such, God didn't do anything without telling Robertson first.

The stealthy, deceptive strategies of the Religious Right should remind us of one thing: despite their growing numbers, the Religious Right is a minority, and always will be. And they know it. That does not, however, minimize their threat. As long as reasonable people do nothing, the Religious Right will continue to do well in low-turnout elections, such as school boards. Their effect that area alone can be devastating.

There are several things concerned citizens can do to challenge the Christian Right. Register to vote. Become informed about the issues. Know the candidates. Vote.

Frederick Clarkson, in *Challenging the Christian Right – The Activist's Handbook*, says, "Opponents of the theocrats are at a disadvantage. For the most part, they know little about them. One can subscribe to the magazines and send for the books, and still not really know what to do to counter them locally. National political organizations are usually limited in what they can do to help. Although it is a struggle that is nationally in scope, it is local in the ways that matter most, whether it is a clinic defense, a school board race, or battling an anti-gay rights initiative."

Therefore, the first thing to do is go to church — in the sense that this is a church-based, theocratic movement. So, one needs to know which churches are involved, and the exact nature of their political beliefs and activities.

If there are churches know to be affiliated with Operation Rescue, or the Christian Coalition, these are good places to start. It is out of such churches that not only voters, but activists and campaign workers, financial contributors, and candidates are most likely to emerge. Thus, to know the network of churches is, to a considerable degree, to know the political movement itself.

The number of churches and "fellowships" will vary from place to place, depending on the size of the community and the extent of the fun-

American Jesus

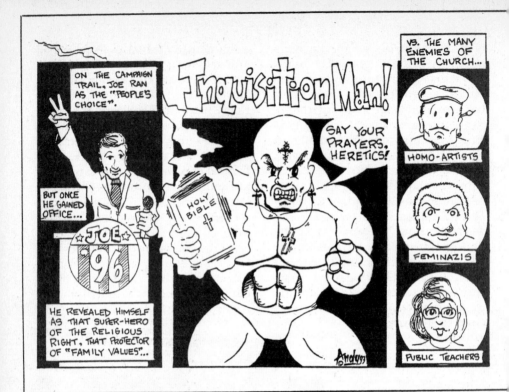

damentalist presence. Some "charismatic" mainstream Protestant and Catholic churches are also worth checking out as possible centers of theocratic thought and action. Other good places to check out are "Christian bookstores," which one can find through the Yellow Pages. Some Christian bookstores have little but pietist literature, candles and greeting cards, but many are also deeply political. Such places are centers for distribution of Christian Right literature, newspapers, magazines, videos, and political notices. If you find such a place, you can begin to figure out who in your community is worth monitoring. "American Opinion " bookstores, which are affiliated with the John Birch Society, are also likely to intersect with the Christian Right, and are worth a visit. Many politically oriented churches have their own bookstores, which often include tape ministries. Usually, this is simply a collection of Sunday sermons and guest speakers. Acquiring such tapes

can offer clues, and a record of the political views and activities of the church. Sometimes one can find local leaders and elected officials on tape.

Once key churches and bookstores in an area have been identified, it is worth stopping by once in a while to see what's new. Churches are often open on Saturday or during the week, and literature can be perused in the lobby of the bookstore. As primary and general elections approach, political activity, including voter registration drives, tend to increase, particularly on Sundays when more people are around.

Clarkson advises, "Find other people who are concerned about the Christian Right with whom you can work, preferably people you know well."

Secondly, you and/or your group should get educated, so you have a more or less common understanding of what's going on. Share interesting news clips and magazine articles. Become conversational with the main players, institutions, and tactics of the Christian Right, locally and nationally. Make a small contribution to a local or national Christian Right organization. This way you get on their mailing list. (If you wish to keep your home address private, rent a post office box.) Additionally, local or state chapters of such groups as Concerned Women for America, or the Christian Coalition, often have their own newsletters.

Sometimes "Christian" radio stations make for interesting listening if you are trying to find out what's going on in your area. Like the Christian bookstores, many are just devotional or music-oriented, but some carry the news and views of the Christian Right. Be on the alert for programming from Pat Robertson's CBN Radio Network, Marlin Maddoux's Radio America, James Dobson's Focus on the Family, the Don Wildmon Report, or Operation Rescue's Randall Terry.

Not long ago, I went to Austin, Texas, to speak to a group about the Religious Right. A woman representing the group picked me up at the airport. On the way into the city we listened to the most popular of several Christian radio stations in the area. Within seconds of turning on the radio, I heard the announcer mention my name, and urge all the good Christians of Austin to show up to protest what I had to say!

In doing your research, keep good files. You will probably find that the various organizations of the Christian Right intersect and that they usually (but not always) work closely together. (Forming a study group can be a good way to begin. See

ad in this issue for information on *Challenging the Christian Right,* written by Frederick Clarkson and myself.)

It is likely that whoever the leaders of the local Christian Right are, they have a track record. There is likely to be more information about them locally than you might think, including in the local newspaper and the library.

Once started, many local groups that are formed to challenge the Religious Right start a newsletter. These contain ongoing information and analysis of the political activities of the local and regional theocrats. A newsletter ensures that with or without the newspapers, the information and analysis you think is important gets out to people who need it, and helps shape the thinking of the political community. This is particularly important if the local press is reluctant to cover the story on an ongoing basis.

In the end, the Religious Right will meet its defeat, not at the hands of any large national organization, but through hundreds, maybe thousands, of local organizations and coalitions that formed to challenge the Christian Right and preserve true democracy.

Skipp Porteous is President and National Director of the Institute for First Amendment Studies (IFAS). IFAS has released the Second Edition of **Challenging the Christian Right** *— The Activist's Handbook. Copies are available for $20, plus $3.50 for P&H. Write to IFAS, Great Barrington, MA 01230.*

Challenging the Christian Right

The Activist's Handbook

Frederick Clarkson and Skipp Porteous have revised and updated their indispensable handbook to include 290 pages of features, profiles, and background material. Through the meticulously researched articles, you'll learn what the goals and agenda of the Religious Right are. What other activist groups are doing to counter theocratic attacks on First Amendment freedoms. How to research the Christian Right in your area. And, the handbook includes extensive reference sections on resource organizations and useful books, profiles of the top ten Christian Right groups, and a state-by-state rundown of the Religious Right.

To get your copy of Challenging the Christian Right

send $20 plus $3.50 shipping and handling ($1.50 s&h for every book thereafter) to Institute for First Amendment Studies, Inc., P.O. Box 589, Great Barrington, MA 01230. Please give street address when ordering. Mass. residents add 5% sales tax.

CHRISTIAN COALITION GEARS UP IN PENNSYLVANIA

Steve Goldstein

The sales pitch is worthy of the best advertising copy-writer.

"Think like Jesus. Lead Like Moses. Fight Like David. Run Like Lincoln," says the brochure of the Christian Coalition Leadership School.

School was to be in session Saturday in Pittsburgh, where television evangelist Pat Robertson was scheduled to launch a major fund-raising drive for the Christian Coalition, which he founded to advance the political aspirations of the religious right.

Moving off the streets and into the government, the coalition is spear-heading the drive against, among other things, abortion, homosexual rights and outcomes-based education.

The strategy is to advance the conservative agenda by training and electing like-minded public officials to decision-making bodies and municipal governments to state and local political committees.

"The real battles of concern to Christians are in neighborhoods, school boards, city councils and state legislatures," Christian Coalition executive director Ralph Reed Jr., who will join Robertson in Pittsburgh, has said.

Nationwide in scope, the coalition's drive is strongly targeted to Pennsylvania, a basically conservative state that has one of the nation's toughest anti-abortion laws.

This weekend marks the first of 12 "intensive training seminars" the Christian Coalition has scheduled for Pennsylvania this year, the most of any state.

The Pennsylvania Christian Coalition was founded a year ago and has helped anti-abortion activists gain as many as half the seats on the state Republican committee, GOP officials say.

That success has created anxiety among some GOP regulars who believe the coalition's agenda does not coincide with the best interests of the state's Republican Party.

"I'm greatly concerned that they are holding so many conferences in Pennsylvania," said John Denny, director of the Republican Future Fund, a political action committee formed to support moderate Republicans who favor abortion rights.

"They are absolutely targeting the GOP in this state. The Christian Coalition is intolerant of other opinions in the party. It's their way or the highway."

Pennsylvania "is one of the hotspot states" where conservative Christian groups are most active, according to Matt Freeman, a director with the Washington-based People for the American Way, a nonpartisan organization that monitors what it perceives as assaults on constitutional liberties by the religious right.

Rick Schenker, executive director of the Pennsylvania Christian

THE RELIGIOUS RIGHT'S PERFECT "STATE" OF AFFAIRS—

RIGHT MAKES RIGHT?

Andy 93

Christian Coalition has prepared and distributed a thick County Action Plan, which the chapter's executive director describes as "a how-to manual for building a real grass-roots organization."

A copy of the County Action Plan manual, obtained by *The Inquirer* and titled with the biblical quote "Come let us rebuild . . . and we will no longer be in disgrace," offers a step-by-step plan for starting a county chapter, registering sympathetic voters, lobbying for "pro-family conservative values" and electing public officials who support these values.

To establish links with the Republican and Democratic Parties, the manual encourages coalition members to run for state and local party committees, the grass-roots political organizations of both parties.

But the manual cautions, "you should never mention the name Christian Coalition in Republican or Democratic circles."

"What concerns me most is not their position on any one issue, but their covert nature," Denny said.

Schenker, author of the manual, said in a recent telephone interview that the document given to *The Inquirer* was a "draft" that had been stolen several months ago during a coalition conference in Virginia Beach, Va.

Coalition, agreed that Pennsylvania was fertile territory for his group.

"People are begging for what we are doing," he said. "Wherever I go people are saying, 'Here's a vehicle for me to get involved.' And they're coming out of the woodwork to do it. I wish I could keep up with it."

The state, Freeman asserted, provides "a relatively hospitable political environment" for the religious right, in part, because of the conservative, rural composition of a large portion of the state. Political strategist James Carville once described Pennsylvania as "Philadelphia and Pittsburgh with Alabama in between."

Since it was formed in February 1992, the Pennsylvania chapter of the

He described the caution about identification as meant not to encourage deception, but to avoid discrimination against coalition members.

The manual has since been revised, Schenker said, in part to remove passages about recruiting and assisting political candidates — activities prohibited by the group's pending application for tax-exempt status.

"We were advised by our lawyers that this wasn't kosher with the IRS laws," said Schenker, "especially because the Christian Coalition was being scrutinized."

He noted that the finished manual had been largely adopted by the national Christian Coalition as a model for other states.

"I wrote the manual as a citizen's tool," he said. "It's a typical American approach to the political process.

"Our goal is to influence public policy, and we need to do that through training and lobbying.

We're doing it from the bottom up. To go for the long bomb — a presidential or U.S. Senate race — is ridiculous."

A monthly newsletter, *The Pennsylvania Reporter*, is being published. The coalition, which has 54 chapters in the state, seeks to have 70 formed by June. With the aid of satellite dishes, it hopes to be able to broadcast programs to the county chapters from national headquarters.

Directors of the Pennsylvania Christian Coalition include former State Rep. Peter Vroon of Chester County; Jerry Bowyer, and accountant from Pittsburgh, and Clay Mankamyer of Somerset County, a former Pennsylvania state trooper and regional field director of the national body.

Asked about Robertson's stated goal of having "working control" of the GOP by 1996, Schenker said:

"We have a huge amount of people we work with in both parties."

Schenker said the Pennsylvania chapter plans to continue to actively oppose abortion as well as any attempt "to add sexual orientation as behavior to civil rights legislation."

At People for the American Way, the coalition's actions are being followed with interest.

Arthur Kropp, president of People for the American Way, said his group's members were concerned chiefly because they believe that the political success of the religious right often has come at the expense of the constitutional rights of others.

And the religious right has had political success, he said.

Kropp said his group had tracked 500 local political races nationwide involving the religious right. By his group's count, the religious right won 40 percent of the time, Kropp said.

Reprinted with permission from the Philadelphia Inquirer

EXOTIC WOMEN!
THE SEXIEST WOMEN IN COMICS!

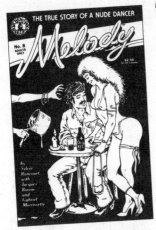

MELODY: Autobiography of a Nude Dancer! Sylvie Rancourt is a nude dancer in Montreal under the stage name "Melody". This ongoing graphic tale recounts her amazing experiences with other dancers, club owners and patrons. How did she get into the business? What is it *like* stripping? What goes on backstage? All here! All true! Illustrated by top Canadian artist Jacques Boivin.

OMAHA the Cat Dancer. Omaha is a hot stripper whose loves, adventure and intrigue have garnered numerous award nominations. Long considered the top X-rated comic book. Featured in *Playboy*, *Hustler* and many men's magazines. Sexy stories by writer Kate Worley and artist Reed Waller.

CHERRY. The sexploits of a blonde bimbo named Cherry Poptart who usually finds a way to get what she wants – and she wants a lot! Loaded with mirth and mayhem! You want your comix with non-stop sex? This is for you! We even have *a 3-D issue* with special glasses for action that pops off the page!! Our most popular title – by Larry and Sharon Welz.

CHERRY! FER CHRISSAKE! WE GOT A FUCKING **SHOW** TO PUT ON!

HEY! 'SSOKAY! I'M FINE! I WAS JUS' TAKIN' A LI'L ⸮HIC!⸵ BRRPP! QUICKIE BREAK, Y'KNOW? TEEHEE!

RONZO HAS AGREED TO BE A JUDGE!

YEAH, BUT WHAT'S HE GONNA **JUDGE**? WE HAVE NO...

I'M PUMPED!

WHOA!

IS THIS THE CONTEST?

WHERE DO I SIGN UP?

ARE WE LATE?

I WANNA ENTER!

WHO'S IN CHARGE?

ME, TOO!

MY BOY-FRIEND MADE ME DO IT!

The Sting of Pornography

Cecil E. Greek, Ph.D.

Both U.S. Customs and the U.S. Postal Inspection Service initiated major sting operations, such as Operation Looking Glass, in the late 1980s, principally aimed at catching those who are inclined to purchase child pornography. The government used a variety of questionable techniques which bordered on entrapment to locate potential customers (Stanley, 1989:323; *W. 57th*, 1988; Howard, 1992).

In 1992, the Supreme Court ruled in a case involving entrapment in these sting operations [*Jacobson v. U.S.*]. Keith Jacobson, a Nebraska farmer, was targeted by the U.S. Postal Inspection Service's Operation Looking Glass because his name was found on a list of those who had previously purchased legal magazines which included nude pictures of boys. As a result, the government spent two and one-half years attempting to entice Mr. Jacobson to purchase illegal child pornography.

No efforts were first made to find out if Mr. Jacobson, or any of the other targeted individuals, were indeed child molesters. According to Chief Postal Inspector Daniel Mahalco, since the distributors of child pornography had all been driven out of the business, the next step was to go after the consumers of such materials, with the ultimate hope that children would now be protected from sexual abuse and molestation [Howard, 1992]. Mahalco reported that of the 160 indicted as a result of Operation Looking Glass, 35 cases of sexual molestation were uncovered. In targeting suspects, the Postal Inspection Service presumed that previous purchase of nude pictures of children was sufficient to prove criminal predisposition to purchase illegal child pornography, which they assumed was collected only by practicing pedophiles. When asked why he had not first checked to find out if Jacobson was a pedophile, Mahalco replied: "We're not going to wait until someone molests a child before we go after him." [Howard, 1992]

The tactics employed against Jacobson were similar to those used against hundreds of other unsuspecting individuals. First, Jacobson was sent a series of letters from a phony organization, the American Hedonist Society, [others employed by the sting included "Research Facts," "Midlands Data Research," "Freedom's Choice," and "Ohio Valley Action League" (Stanley, 1989:323)] claiming to be a First Amendment Sexual Libertarian group out to stop government censorship. If a targeted individual responded to the mailing, they were then sent questionnaires and surveys regarding their interests. For example, Heartland Institute for a New Tomorrow sent Jacobson a survey, claiming they were trying to gauge the public's interest in the repeal of all statutes regarding nonviolent sexual activities, including removing age limitations. In addition, HINT claimed to be involved in lobbying efforts, and hoped to interest Jacobson in purchasing fund raising items from a forthcoming catalog, hinting that porn might be available.

Those that returned the surveys were then offered pen pals who shared their interests. While Jacobson never responded to the pen pal request, a number of other men did. Those that did were given pen pals. Sometimes male postal inspectors pretended to be young sexually adventurous mothers recently divorced or widowed, who hinted that they were looking for a relationship with an older man and that their children might be available for photographs. Some of the men became quite infatuated with these young women who seemed to be so interested in them, and lipstick stained letters were not uncommon. Postal inspectors also pretended to be the young daughters of "sexually liberated" mothers who wanted to ask their new special "uncle" intimate questions about sex. In general, the phony letters employed a technique known as "mirroring," with the postal/customs agents attempting to reflect whatever the interests were of the persons they had contacted. Sometimes pen pals even offered to trade child pornography with the targeted individuals.

After two and one-half years of such solicitations from both postal inspectors and the U.S. Custom Service's "Operation Borderline," Jacobson, mostly out of curiosity, ordered a magazine containing child pornography from one of the catalogs offered by the Far East Trading Company. During this time period the only such catalogs going through the mails were those of the government, the only known commercial outlet for such materials [Stanley, 1989]. When the magazine arrived at Jacobson's house he was immediately

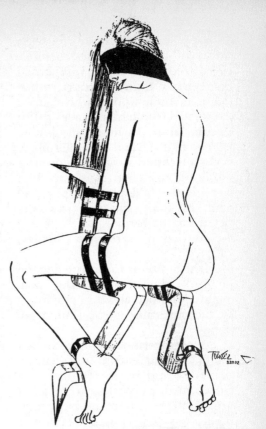

arrested; a search of his house found no other child pornography. He was later convicted and served his sentence.

Five of the 160 indicted as a result of Operation Looking Glass committed suicide rather than face the embarrassment of public exposure. These included Robert Brase, Thomas Cleasby, Gary Hester, and Dale Riva.

A very interesting case was that of 61-year-old Rev. John Zangger. He believed that circumcision was an unbiblical practice and devoted a considerable amount of time to speaking out against it. In order to demonstrate his belief, Zangger collected a series of slides from a research project which included photos of uncircumcised boys' penises and had these enlarged and transferred to videotape. In addition, he made a tape of himself masturbating his uncircumcised penis. With these tapes he hoped to demonstrate the superiority of noncircumcised penises. He shared these tapes with Postal Inspector Calvin Comfort, a.k.a. Jolene, a young woman who claimed she wanted to join his crusade against circumcision. In addition, Jolene feigned that she had become romantically interested in the reverend after watching his tape. Zangger then faced both child pornography and adult obscenity charges, was convicted for the former, but later had the conviction overturned [Swadey, 1993].

The Supreme Court ruled in the Jacobson decision that the techniques described above as employed by the government constituted entrapment:

The Government did not establish that the defendant, who had received mailings from the Government purporting to be from organizations asserting individual rights, was predisposed to commit the offense prior to first contact by the Government . . . Government did not establish that defendant had a predisposition, independent of government action, to receive child pornography through the mail where evidence showed that he was ready and willing to commit the offense only after Government had engaged in two and one-half years of undercover activity consisting of communications from fictitious organizations and persons attempting to convince defendant that he had the right or should have the right to engage in behavior proscribed by law [*Jacobson v. U.S.*, 1992:1535].

Nevertheless, the result of the these increased efforts in the late 1980s were greater numbers of investigations, arrests, and convictions for child pornography. Arrests made by the Postal Inspector peaked at 314 in 1988. Statistics on child pornography as supplied by the U.S. Post Office appear below.

Child Pornography Cases: U.S. Postal Inspector

YEAR	1,987	1,988	1,989	1,990	1,991
Cases Initiated	406	214	225	319	N/A
Cases on Hand (end of FY)	549	494	477	564	533
Cases Closed	211	440	280	233	N/A
Federal Arrests	206	234	123	145	93
State Arrests	36	80	56	58	59
Federal Convictions	149	248	147	144	110
State Convictions	45	53	56	54	35
Total Declinations	8	20	24	25	23

Source: U.S. Postal Inspection Service

While virtually no one would support the use of children in the making of pornographic photos or videos, little is actually known, despite the above arrest and conviction figures, about the extent of such practices in the contemporary United States. However, since the alleged dangers to children played such an important part of 1986 Meese Commission testimony and findings, it is not surprising that Congress also reacted to the Meese report by attempting to pass new legislation aimed at stiffening laws regarding child pornography and that law enforcement officials stepped up their efforts in this area. In 1988, Congress passed the "Child Protection and Obscenity Enforcement Act". The bill's title is somewhat ironic, given that child pornography is not protected by the First Amendment [See NY v. Ferber, 1982; Osborne v. Ohio, 1990] and it is neither professionally manufactured nor sold commercially in the America [Stanley, 1988]. (Child pornography is either imported from overseas or nonprofessionally produced by pedophiles who trade such materials with each other.) In reality, this bill was principally aimed at making sure that underaged performers, such as Traci Lords, are not allowed to pass themselves off as adults [National Obscenity Enforcement Unit, 1988:10-11]. To insure compliance the law required proof that all the actors/models in a pornographic film or magazine were of legal age (18) at the time of the performance or photographing. The bill made the proof requirements retroactive, meaning that all photographs taken over the previous ten years, if they were still being commercially distributed, must have records to verify the ages of performers. The adult video industry's lobbying group (the Adult Video Association) joined with the mainstream publishing and film industries to oppose the bill, but it was passed anyway [Greek, 1989; Margold, 1989]. However, the bill was later found unconstitutional by the courts in 1989 [American Library Association v. Thornburgh] on the basis that the record-keeping provisions were too broad and overly burdensome, and posed a serious potential that persons not engaged in child pornography would be convicted [DeWitt, 1991:24]. In 1990, Congress reenacted the legislation, attempting to rectify the criticisms made in American Library Association. The revised law — The Child Protection Restoration and Penalties Enhancement Act — was also contested and struck down by a district court in Washington, D.C. in May 1992 on grounds similar to the first case.

The Child Protection and Obscenity Enforcement Act of 1988 was in fact the fourth piece of antipornography legislation passed by Congress since 1977, all enacted to eliminate child pornography—The Protection of Children Against Child Exploitation Act of 1977, The Child Protection Act of 1984, and The Child Sexual Abuse and Pornography Act of 1986 were the others [von Raab, 1986; Stanley, 1989:302]. A resulting paradox is that in a great many jurisdictions, teenagers have the full legal right to consent to sexual intercourse, but they may not legally consent to be photographed in a lascivious pose [Stanley, 1989:307]. Federal and state efforts at redefining what is "child pornography" have gone so far that many parents now fear taking nude pictures of their own children lest they be turned in by the photo processor, who is now required to report suspicious negatives [Andriette, 1991].

One of the most severe critics of the recent child porn campaigns is Lawrence Stanley. According to Stanley [1989:295], the production and

commercial distribution of child pornography had been virtually eliminated when the first new federal law took effect in 1978, yet "kiddy porn" continued to be exploited nationwide by law enforcement officials, moral crusaders, politicians, and the media anyway as a grave social danger. "Kiddy porn" was employed repeated as a rhetoric to justify new antipornography legislation in the 1980s [D'Emilio and Freedman, 1988:353]. Among the unsubstantiated claims made concerning pornographic exploitation of children were of: "child auctions in Amsterdam, toll-free numbers and mail-order houses for ordering child prostitutes, child 'snuff' films, satanic molestation rituals in which animals are dismembered, 'chains of American brothels and bordellos where children were kept under lock and key', and motorcycle gang rapes" [Stanley, 1989:309]. A number of the unsubstantiated claims regarding child pornography by "child abuse experts"

such as Judianne Densen-Gerber [1979, 1980] and Shirley O'Brien [1983] were uncritically accepted by the Meese Commission and included as fact in the report (See also [*NBC News*, 1985]). Alfred Regnery [1985:5], then head of OJJDP, made the outlandish claim that child pornography represented a one-half to one billion dollars a year industry.

In the early 1980s, the hysteria over child pornography merged with the "missing children" scare — which also later proved to be unfounded [Best, 1990]. In addition, claims about child pornography were sometimes attached to Fundamentalist legends regarding Satanism. A number of criminologists and sociologists of religion (Lyons [1988], Alexander [1990], Carlson and Larue [1989], Hicks [1991], Best [1990], Lanning [1990], Victor [1990], and Richardson et al [1991]) have argued that Christian fundamentalists — along with talk show hosts like Geraldo Rivera [1989] — have helped to give credence to a number of urban myths concerning a major upsurge in Satanic activity, including the following: young women — "breeders" — who are forced to give birth to hundreds of babies annually which are then sacrificed to Satan and cannibalized; daycare centers that covertly double as Satanic covens practicing ritualistic sexual abuse of children, including the production of child pornography; and a conspiracy of police, lawyers, judges, and politicians hiding such practices from discovery. (For discussion of why right-wing Christians sometimes accept such conspiracy theories see Toch [1965:45-85] and Johnson [1983:163-186].) Judith Reisman [1991:133-136], for example, has claimed that ritualistic abuse and murder of children is advocated by magazines such as *Playboy*. She alleged that 10% of *Playboy*'s cartoons feature killing, maiming, or murdering of children, thus linking pornography and Satanism. Reisman [1991:135] has also attacked the works of artists Robert Mapplethorpe and Andres Serrano as that of "satanic pornographers" and testified in the 1990 Cincinnati Mapplethorpe trial. No tapes, films, or photos produced by Satanic child-abusing rings and cults have ever been located [Stanley, 1988].

It was in this context that the Post Office designed their sting operation, yet another incidence of how law enforcement overreacts to public and political pressure to solve crime at all costs, including subverting the Constitution.

Cecil Greek is Assistant Professor of Criminology at the University of South Florida. **Porn Wars: A comparison of American and British Antipornography Campaigns in the 1980s,** *co-authored with William Thompson, will be published by Aldine de Gruyter in 1994.*

NUDE, FUCKED AND FREEZING

Working conditions of the X-rated actor

Wally Anne Wharton

As a free-lance journalist and showgirl of questionable financial means, I am ever vacillating between studio sanctified show biz and so-called "pornographic" entertainment. One day I'm selling cereal and the next day I'm selling my skimpily-clad body. I never linger too long in any one camp; to limit oneself to a single form of exhibitionism would be creative suicide.

What lurks behind mainstream movies and T.V? Superstar romance and movie mogul magic? Try catered meatloaf and trailer life. Between takes actors retreat into their trailers. The bigger the star, the bigger the isolated, brain-deadening trailer.

I haven't seen a trailer once on a sex set. This isn't to say that the end result is better than *Star Wars*, but surely Spartan working conditions and the lack of privacy forces both cast and crew to kindle a real rapport. Or do they?

Recently I interviewed several horizontal harbingers of heavy-breathing on the subject of working conditions in The Underground:

LACY ROSE: I love my work, but sometimes it gets to be a drag if I'm doing a lesbo scene and the other girl's not really into me eating her pussy. I know no matter what I do, I'm turning her off.

NICK EAST: At first I couldn't stand doing anal (sex scenes). It really grossed me out. I had to shut my eyes and fantasize about something else. Now it's okay. I can get it up for two or three scenes in one day, no problem. That's my job. But I can't come gobs; in fact, I can't even make a woman gag . . . I like to use a lot of lube. Why not? I make everything easier. Some actors don't like to use it. It's an ego-thing. They're insulted if their partner isn't naturally dripping wet for forty-five minutes.

TIANNA TAYLOR: Once I had to shoot a (video) box cover and it was freezing cold! They sprayed down my red dress with water because the photographer wanted it to cling to my body. Well, it sure did cling; and the cold made my nipples really hard so the pictures turned out great.

BILL MARGOLD: I have the distinction of being the only person ever to stand in for The King, the late great John Holmes. In January of 1977, I was working both as an actor and an agent and I'd hired Holmes for this film *Phantasm Comes Again* in which he's supposed to do two girls in a swimming pool. John calls me from the set, right in the middle of shooting and says they forgot to heat the pool so forget it. I rush down to the set; they throw a blonde wig on me to try to disguise me as a lifeguard. Then the girls say: "Gee, that first guy was cute but *this* guy is even cuter!" I get into the pool, the girls go at it and my body turns completely numb. I get off but don't feel a thing. And my skin turns bright purple. Two weeks later, John actually returned the $250 I'd paid him. That was rare. The King was incredibly cheap.

Aside from occasionally fucking in sub-zero temperatures, what other health risks must porn performers endure? What about safe sex and the use of condoms? I spoke about this touchy subject director John D. Player, curator of young talent and creator of the infamous biker-porn series *The Adventures of Dirty Harry.*

JOHN PLAYER: I'm in the business to entertain. My actors have to be willing to take a risk or they're in the wrong profession. If go to a circus I don't want to see the guy on the trapeze tethered to a dozen bungi cords with trampolines and fireman waiting down below and a big balloon tied to his ass. What fun is that?

W. W.: A balloon tied to his ass might be fun.

PLAYER: You know what I mean. Who wants to see a stunt man doing something that doesn't look dangerous? So if some new actress wants to use rubbers I say no. Besides, the guy always comes in her face anyway. But if Hypatia Lee wants to use rubbers, she can do what she wants because she's a star and people will still buy her movies. But I *do* make people wear rubbers for anal scenes; getting trich is worse than getting AIDS any day.

I'm about to play a small part in my second John Leslie film, *Anything that Moves.* Get it? I arrive at a run-down Hollywood hip-hop club that looks even more run-down in the harsh daylight. Two hundred feet before the entrance I'm already tripping over cables. Leslie doesn't shoot on tape; he shoots on film. This makes for a much costlier production and a much longer day for cast and crew.

There's a certain mood on an X-rated set. It's irreverent and high-spirited; it's in-your-ass audacity. It says the whole world trots off to boring jobs everyday while we tape naked women for a living.

I am well-trained talent: First I check in with the A.D. (assistant director) and production manager. In a Leslie production, even these chores go to adult entertainment legends like Jamie Gillis and Henri Packard. Willis growls and smirks characteristically while checking my name off his clipboard. Packard (also co-writer of the script) smiles at me myopically and shows me the way to the girls' bathroom which doubles as the dressing room. There is an alcove where the make-up man and hairdresser have set up their hot curlers and paint boxes, but these are only

for the principal players — only those who "screw."

Lunch has come and gone but I notice that a generous table of coffee, snacks and soft drinks remains to placate the extras. So far conditions seem as adequate as at any "B" movie shoot. However, as I hit the bathroom I'm met with a glaring reminder that this is a fuck film, not Masterpiece Theater. Scattered all

> "There's a certain mood on an X-rated set. It's irreverent and high-spirited; it's in-your-ass audacity."

over the floor, on the sink, next to the toilets, is a plethora of Masengill Douche paraphernalia and box after box of contraceptive sponges. Evidently the actresses have a safe sex agenda of their own. Scavenger that I am, I check the expiration date on the Nonoxynol-9 and stuff a couple unopened sponges into my purse. Hey, you never know.

A strip sequence is filmed utilizing the many porn fan extras. These guys may or may not be paid. Some fans will do anything to be near their favorite female performers. Most of them fit the misfit category: wimpy, lonely guys with too much fat and too many problems to handle a real relationship with a woman. I talk one little guy with a hairlip into giving me a picture he's taken of me at the Fans of X-Rated Entertainment, or

F.O.X.E. awards. It's like taking candy from a baby.

Red lights and dry ice simulate a smoke-filled late-night strip joint. A sequined, baby-faced Tracy Winn removes her bra and steps out of her G-string. No music plays as she undulates; that'll be dubbed in later, but her spectators' lust is real.

Originally I'm hired for a non-speaking role but one of the strippers doesn't show up so Pachard takes a second look at my cleavage and elevates my performing status. I am assigned one unforgettable incomplete sentence: "Kiss niggers." Before we shoot I introduce myself to the three other actresses plus Leslie's favorite star, Selena Steele. I remind her that I've met her before on sets and at various awards ceremonies and she warms up a little. Just a little. Helena is a major force in this industry and she doesn't have to be nice to anyone.

Our scene is full of harsh words, pushing and shoving — even fake blood. After all, watching girls fight is a popular fetish. Leslie blocks our moves and injects us with plenty of energy, but he seems content with mediocre acting abilities. I am "wrapped." Henri Pachard beefs up my check for the added contribution. I thank him and leave, eschewing the sex scene. I'm not in the mood to fight the fans for a good view. Plus, filming a single sex scene to film on 16mm could take several hours.

There's plenty of good, clean sex to see during the F. J. Lincoln production of *Girl Trouble*. This time I'm not acting; I'm merely observing a prominent porn director at work. Taped at Henri Pachard's comfortable San Fernando home, I'd feel like I was at a barbecue if it weren't for the huge black cables snaking their way across every inch of the white shag carpet. Lincoln's wife and collaborator Patti Rhodes arranges snacks and soft drinks in the kitchen. Actress Heather Hart relaxes in curlers and a bathrobe. Woody Long is joking with the crew. Ebony beauty Dominique Simone plays up her huge green eyes with long, light brown hair that must have washing instructions sewn in the back.

Superstud Marc Wallice collects his gear into a duffle bag and prepares to leave. I make a mad dash to catch him. Wallice is so good-looking that he's an irritant to many male viewers who write into video magazines to ball-bash him. Any guy that brings out the cattiness in men must be worth meeting. Marc looks and talks like he's never had a rough day in his life and I mean this in a positive way. I ask for his number and *get it*. What a coup!

Five actresses in various stages of undress and high heels rehearse their orgy, known in the porn world as a "daisy chain." For the next half hour Lincoln hones his vision of sexual perfection. He's not adverse to shooting again and again if he feels the sequence can be improved upon. As a director, John Leslie sometimes gets a little irritated at the crew if things don't go his way. Lincoln has the patience of Job.

Finally the girls suck, lick and plunder each others' bodies with dildos to Lincoln's specifications.

"OOOhhhh, yeah, fuck me baby, heahhhhhh!!" shouts one tanned, climactic blonde.

"And . . . cut," says Fred. "Great. Okay, girls take a break while we set up the next shot."

The girls rush by, flushed and giggly.

"Boy, was that wonderful!" says Lincoln, all smiles as he takes a long sip of water and tosses his wild mane of gray. "The blonde was fuckin' her and then she got off and then the other girl came. Whoa, that was hot!" Can't he tell they were totally faking it? I hesitate to burst his misconstrued male bubble and instead, nod in complete agreement. Spineless, that's what I am.

I return to the set later that evening. Patti Rhodes treats myself and a few other industry spectators to a cold flute of champagne. Now this is *my* kind of movie shoot! My editor from *Hustler Erotic Video Guide*, Scott Mallory, is gearing up for his classic portrayal of a male chauvinist pig. He glances at a bare-bones script in between trading one-liners with Fred, Patti and myself.

Soon Fred and Mal O'Ree are upstairs with the two leading ladies, one of whom is shooting for the very first time. I watch downstairs on the monitor to avoid the unbearably hot lights. The two actresses avenge Mal O'Ree's character's sexist ways by tying him up in their lingerie and making love right in front of him. Mat O' Ree squirms and the gals rub their sticky bodies up against his helplessly

hard cock. That'll teach him who's boss. Why doesn't the women's movement try this one? The neophyte shoves her pink panties in Mal O'Ree's mouth like a gag. Later I find out it was an ad-lib.

It's nearly midnight. Everyone's exhausted and Pachard's (now-ex) wife is ragging on everyone to get the hell out of her house. Lincoln remains undaunted, slowly, carefully getting the footage he needs. Finally he presents his two "eating ladies" with huge bouquets of roses and poses for press pictures with a naked girl perched on each of his thighs holding flowers, beauty-pageant style.

I'm doing a video called *Hung in the Balance*. Gay porn at it's finest. As the only woman in an all-male extravaganza, I feel like Carol Channing.

The Trusdale locale is a sprawling late sixties ranchstyle with a terrific view of Benedict Canyon. It

*Set of **Fantasy Exchange**: Actress Nikki Sinn   Photo: Wally Wharton*

Wally Wharton and director Henri Pachard
Photo: Randy Spears

belongs to an older gay couple; two old queens who made good.

I'm the first to arrive.

"They're going to be a little late," says one of the owners. "They're changing locations." He shows me to a small back bedroom with a spotlessly clean bathroom attached.

I change into my favorite outfit first, in hope that the director will say, "That's fine." I suppose if I didn't bring anything else they'd have to go with my only costume but I like to give the director a choice. Directors love choices. Plus, it makes me look co-operative and it gives me a chance to show off my wardrobe.

An hour later the crew piles in. Director Hector (not his real name), a sensitive-looking Latino, begins setting the table and speaking in hushed tones to the cameraman. Chicken arrives that we can't eat because it's prop food.

I play Katherine, former wife of could-pass-for-straight "Chad" who is now living with overtly-gay "Tad." "Chad" invites me for dinner and I wreak havoc between the two lovers by being bitchy, glib, and still hot for my ex-husband. An X-rated gay "Falcon Crest. "

I emerge from the back bedroom and show Hector my outfit, a low-cut pink fushia spaghetti-strap from Trashy Lingerie. Hector's face clouds while the other actors applaud.

"I figured this is a skin flick so I'd show some skin," I remark weakly .

"Oh yes, honey, show it to us!" someone shouts.

"It's wrong for the scene," says Hector. "Let's see what else you've got. And take off some of that eye make-up."

We finally settle on a purple knit suit. Good thing I brought that turtleneck dickey so I can cover up my offensive mammary glands.

I sit down at the table, suddenly very aware of my gender. I decide not to butt into the conversation. The boys are chatting like magpies. Perhaps the only true benefit of being an L.A. actor is hanging out with other actors and talking about how fucked up being an actor is. Prettyboy "Chad" is living in Malibu with the producer who has a rep for befriending young gay actors. Hmm....

There is a script, but Hector tells me I won't need one. He either feeds us lines or we ad-lib. The actors are amazingly proficient, more so than in straight X productions. "Tad" has great comic timing and facial expressions. Hector stops us often, very concerned with character motivation and subtext. I feel like an actress again. However, I can tell that leading man "Chad" is feeling pressured and a little unrehearsed.

"I'm sorry," he says to me. "Can we start again? I keep forgetting your character's name."

"M-my name is Katherine," I warble in my best Parkinsonian Hepburn. "How could you-oo forge-et?"

That breaks the ice. We wail on the scene and have a little time left over to nibble the cold chicken.

I forget my Reeboks and go back the next afternoon to retrieve them. All the guys are literally prancing around in their BVDs. They have just finished a sex scene.

"Oh, Wall!"

"Hi, Wally."

"Hi guys! I'm just here to get my shoes."

"Listen, Wally," says Hector, squiring me into the conversation pit. "I think you're really good. I have to direct a scene for my directing class at UCLA. Would you be in it for me?"

"Sure," I reply, momentarily flattered into forgetting all the hours of unpaid inconvenient rehearsal ahead.

"Good," says Hector, clearly relieved. We set up a schedule for the following week. Suddenly he looks nervous again. "But please don't tell anyone in the class we did this movie together. I don't want anyone to know I direct porn."

Some malcontents like Hector desperately want to move on to a more legitimatized cinematic medium. Others such as Fred Lincoln and John Leslie wear their scarlet X proudly. To adult entertainment performers, the drawbacks of a limited budget are secondary to the thrill of having sex on film. Movies, television, straight porn, gay porn; it's all one big show business carnival. I admire all who participate in any capacity. Those who say, "Watch me sing! Watch me dance! Watch me do a double penetration!" are a rare breed. Maybe not so rare in Hollywood.

---

*Wally Wharton, the self-proclaimed "Thinking Man's Bimbo," has a monthly column in hustler **Erotic Video Guide** entitled "Wally's Whack World!" Often referred to as a female Will Rogers in latex, Wharton is also the author of a humor book that needs a publisher with the balls to take on **Dating for Dollars — a Girl's Guide to Greed.***

Imagine creating your perfect lover. The person who embodies all your desires.

MAKING LOVE

A novel of sex and horror

Bram Stoker award-winning authors Melanie Tem and Nancy Holder team up to bring you MAKING LOVE, a sensually terrifying tale inspired by Mary Shelley's Frankenstein.

When Charlotte Tobias learns she can create the man of her dreams, she has no idea that he will end up to be her worst nightmare. He awakens her and changes her. He takes her to the edge of her fantasies. And now he has taken control. He is all hunger and fury. *And he is without a soul.*

Dell

THE EROTIC ELEVEN

Bobby Lilly

I attended the 1993 Las Vegas Consumer Electronic Show (CES) last January with my spouses, Dave and Nina Hartley. As an adult actress, Nina had a full schedule that week; but, she volunteered to perform at a benefit to raise money for the adult industry's battle against censorship.

The benefit, a lingerie show, was held for the third year in a row at the Pure Pleasure Video Store. Admission was the purchase of a $10 raffle ticket which could be used for any raffle that evening. Additional tickets could also be purchased. Performers modeled lingerie donated by the store and there was a special "gimmick". Winners claimed their lingerie by peeling it off the star's body with their teeth, hands behind their backs at all times.

Friday night Nina attended a rehearsal for The Adult Video News Awards (she was presenting) then went straight to the benefit. About 11:30 that night the phone rang in our room, it was a close friend who had gone to the benefit. The first words out of his mouth were, "Bobby, I want you to know everything's OK and Nina's alright." My heart stopped. Suddenly, my imagination raced out of control and images of "freak" accidents flashed before my eyes. I almost missed his next words. "The show was busted and Nina's been arrested along with everyone else."

Dave immediately headed to the police station. I waited for calls.

When Dave finally checked back, I learned that the eleven performers still at the show (several women had already left) had been arrested and charged with open and gross lewdness, conspiracy to commit prostitution and soliciting prostitution (all misdemeanor charges). The women charged were Nina Hartley, Sharon Mitchell, Patricia Kennedy, Trixi Tyler, Beatrice Valle, Nina Suave, Lacy Rose, Shalene, Danielle Cheeks, Ari, and Naughty Angel.

Bill Margold, head of Fans Of X-rated Entertainment (F.O.X.E.) and the benefit's promoter, was arrested along with the bookstore owner. Seymour Butts, who had videotaped the show, was also arrested. They were charged with multiple counts of felony pandering and receiving money from a prostitute.

The arrests were only made after at least six police officers sat through four hours of live performances. Apparently, they had nothing better to do! They could have stopped the show at any time. Yet, when Capt. Ron Niemann, commander of the vice detail was asked why his detectives didn't act sooner, he was quoted in the Las Vegas Review Journal as saying, "I'm not going to even respond to that. That's stupid. If we had stopped earlier, we wouldn't have gotten all the suspects, would we have?"

Niemann did not explain why, even though fifteen women had performed, only the eleven women present at the end of the evening were

Nina Hartley of the infamous Erotic Eleven being carted off to jail

throughout the show. True? I strongly doubt it.

Reports I heard said several women got carried away on stage and had essentially "woman"-handled a couple of the men from the audience. I was also told that the women had only simulated activity with these men. The only consistent story I got from people who were in the audience is that most of the women appeared to be "playing" with each other. Simulated activity or real — I don't know. Nina, herself, gave a lecture on how to make love to a woman while two friends demonstrated the techniques she described.

Perhaps some of these women did step beyond the bounds of propriety during their performances, but charges of prostitution were totally inappropriate and nothing more than an attempt to hurt and discredit all of them. The police knew *they were performing at a benefit* and should have known they had volunteered to appear on stage that evening. The police had no evidence that the women were paid for *anything* they did that night; but, justified the wholesale prostitution charges by theorizing that the purchase of raffle tickets at the time of admission was actually payment for sexual favors. They also

ever arrested or charged. Nor did he mention why none of the men from the audience who had gotten on stage with the women were arrested. To me, that smacks of sexism and gender discrimination. I am outraged that the police targeted such a benefit. Who was being hurt? Where was the harm to society?

I have been asked what *really* happened that night and have to answer truthfully — I don't know. I wasn't there. However some of the stories I read in the adult press gave the impression that the event was a wild sex orgy where the performers were kept busy servicing the men in the audience one after another insinuated to the press that deals were made ahead of time to rig the raffles. A ludicrous idea if I ever heard one. While the fantasy of appearing on stage with an adult video star may be stimulating, the reality of stepping in front of 800 men who are watching every move you make is terrifying. I can't imagine anyone paying for that experience. Talk about performance anxiety!

I have become a defense coordinator for the women (they have a different lawyer than the men because of possible conflicts of interest) and have been working closely with their attorney, Dominic Gentile. I started a defense fund called THE FREEDOM FUND to cover the actresses' legal fees and expenses. I promised Margold and Butts that, if I raised enough money for the women, I would try to help them as well, but said my first priority was the women.

Arraignments were scheduled for early February but postponed. Deputy District Attorney John Lukens, head of the city's sexual assault unit, was assigned to this case after specifically asking for it (something that is normally never done). He decided to drop the original misdemeanor charges against the women and, instead, filed felony charges with the Clark County Grand Jury under Nevada's ICAN statute, an archaic statute which criminalizes all same sex sexual activity (even in private) and defines such contact as "an infamous crime against nature". It carries a penalty of up to six years in prison.

Obviously, this case has been politicized. Vegas has decided to clean up its "Sin City" image and become more family-oriented. And, Vegas politicians were out to make an example of these women to insure that this *never* happens again.

Butts, the videographer who taped the show, voluntarily appeared before the Grand Jury and turned over his tapes of the event. Charges against him were dropped but indictments were handed down against everyone else on February 26th. The store owner as well as Margold (who also MCed the show) still face multiple counts of pandering. Ten women were each indicted for two counts of "felony lesbianism" for violating Nevada's ICAN Statute and face up to twelve years in jail. One count was for being the active partner and the other for accepting the attentions of her partner. Nina was charged with one count of pandering for ". . . unlawfully, willfully, knowingly and feloniously . . ." encouraging two women ". . . to continue to engage in prostitution by soliciting money from male patrons . . ."

Nina is my "wife." Both at a personal and a political level I am appalled that she was singled out for pandering when all that she did was give a lecture on how to make love to a woman. I believe singling her out in this way was done deliberately to get at this high profile crusader against censorship and discredit her and her cause in the public's eye.

Why did Lukens drop the prostitution charges? If he believed these women were engaged in such activity, why did he drop those charges when charging the women with felony lesbianism? Did he believe he could sway a jury more easily to convict them by inflaming homophobic prejudices? When he dropped the prostitution charges, why did he keep the pandering charges? If there was no prostitution, where was the pandering? Explain his logic — if you can.

Watching this case develop as a member of the immediate family of one of the defendants, I find myself living a nightmare that most people will never know. The stress on all of us is unbelievable. The women know they will have to return to Las Vegas time after time before this case is over. But, they don't know when — and it makes it difficult to schedule work. Their lives are no longer their own; they are subject to the whims of the Nevada court system.

All of us, caught up in this witch-hunt, feel trapped. To stand there helpless, when the power of the state is poised to attack you or someone you love affects the very fabric of your daily life. The emotional stress has caused all of us to act in ways that are not normal. Meaningless arguments over trivia break out and it takes a great deal of restraint not to let them escalate. The on-going stress that we are living with drives ordinary thoughts out of our minds, yet life must go on. Everyone's emotions are stretched to the breaking point. At times I find myself close to tears for no rational reason or losing concentration at times when I need to be focused. The lawyer has become one of the most important persons in our lives. A call from him can make or break our day. All our plans for the next few months are subject to change — and, all our plans are dependant on developments in the case.

Because the police gave the real names and home addresses of these women to the press (not a standard practice), several women have been harassed at home by the media. The women feel personally threatened because their real names and the cities in which they live have been in papers across the country; and, some of them have obsessive fans.

Arraignment had been scheduled for March 12th. According to Nevada State law all criminal cases must be randomly assigned to a trial judge. However, when our case was assigned, all four of that day's cases wound up with the same judge,

Thomas A. Foley, a middle-aged, white, Catholic conservative. The odds against this happening were over 38,000 to 1. Was Foley's assignment just a coincidence or was it politically motivated?

When Dominic Gentile, the women's lawyer, learned this, he took the issue to the Nevada Supreme Court and the scheduled arraignment was stayed. Oral arguments on the issue of the judge's assignment were heard on June 15th. As of early July, the Court had not yet issued a ruling on the matter. The women and their families continue to wait — not knowing when the women will be arraigned or when they will finally have their day in court. The uncertainty of the outcome hangs over all our heads. And, too often, helpless to affect the course of events, we can only wait for an end to the suspense.

Legal fees are mounting and could easily reach six figures. Meetings with the attorney, court appearances, as well as benefit appearances (all for free of course) disrupt our lives and the women have been hurt financially. Nina, like the others, has had to cancel, reschedule and pass up work because she needs to be available. Some of the women have found that they are just not getting as much work as before and some have been told that clubs are afraid to hire them because of possible police surveillance.

It hasn't helped that the industry itself has not been whole-hearted in its support for this case. Some people in the industry are extremely unhappy with the performers and blame them for what happened. They are afraid that this case undermines the Adult Industry's attempts to gain respectability. "How could the women be so stupid as to get themselves into such a situation?" they ask? One company head reportedly said in a meeting of producers and directors who were discussing the case that, if it was up to him, these women would never work again in the industry. He is not alone in his sentiments.

Unfortunately, none of the women's critics seem to realize that what the women did on stage that night was no different than what they could have done legally in any adult video. While the women may have violated Las Vegas' rules, what they did was nothing of which to be ashamed. I know some critics were reacting automatically to the smear word "prostitution." Others were just worried about the case's notoriety; afraid that it would focus negative attention on the adult video industry which was already under assault.

Unfortunately, many of the women do not feel a sense of solidarity with the two men still charged. They feel betrayed, misled and exploited. These women believe Margold and the store owner misled them as to what the safe limits were in that venue (some of the women believe it was done deliberately while others believe it was just incompetence).

These women routinely perform around the country and respect the limits of the venues in which they perform. They depend on the owner of the club or show producer to let them know what is allowed. Unfortunately, Margold and the store owner told the women they could do whatever they felt comfortable doing. And, these women have a wide range of comfort around public sexuality. I must note that neither man produces such shows on a regular basis and Bill told me he didn't realize that he had such a responsibility. He said that he'd had no problems in the past with other shows so didn't expect the police to give him any trouble this time.

For me that's not good enough. People who take a leadership role in the battle against censorship of sexual expression need to think things through more carefully. Anyone producing a high profile benefit like this should have carefully checked and known what the community's limits were from the very beginning. Flouting the law should never happen without a clear, deliberate decision to do so. Everyone had the right to know exactly what they were getting into. Performing at a benefit for freedom of expression does not grant people license to do whatever they want. Strategically, this was not a very intelligent way to fight censorship.

Because of this disaster, the chill of self-censorship has settled over F.O.X.E. Their awards show this past February was extremely tame with no nudity allowed. Afraid the show might have been targeted by law enforcement, many performers decided not to appear or, if they performed, were extremely cautious. Bill says at his next benefit the audience will only get close enough to the stars to throw marshmallows. Hit a star - win a prize.

Anyone who wants to contribute to the women's defense fund can make checks out to THE FREEDOM FUND and mail them to me at 2550 Shattuck Ave, #51, Berkeley, CA 94704.

Bobby Lilly is the founder and Chairperson for Californians Against Censorship Together (CAL-ACT). She will update this report in the next issue of Gauntlet.

Ideas and Thoughts . . .

Eban Lehrer

I am a california-born artist. I paint from my feelings and the feelings around me. I want to share what I see and feel. I feel as if I am on a journey that I know not where it will end.

I am fascinated by the female form and see it as the epitome of beauty. (Beauty . . . That which can be soft . . . That which can be stark or harsh.) As my vision evolves, I begin to explore issues that deal with a woman's own feelings and views of her beauty and sexuality.

I am disturbed and a little scared by the topsy-turvy perceptions of beauty and violence in our culture. The glorification of violence can be evidenced even in the arts (movies, etc.). On the other hand, the human body is seen as something that needs to be covered up and censored.

By comparison, in many other cultures, the human body is seen as something beautiful and violence is seen as obscene. To abhor the celebration of our bodies and embrace the violence done against them sickens me.

I am saddened and concerned by the current big stink surrounding art in terms of obscenity and our bodies. In our society, it is customary to give flowers to show love/like/friendship/appreciation . . . I wonder how many people realize they are giving or receiving the sexual organs of plants! Subtle and not-so-subtle references to our sexuality occur everywhere (just look at advertising).

On the other hand, when listening to some members of our elected government, one gets the idea that anything that does not conform to their ideals (especially that which deals specifically with our sexuality) is dangerous and should be censored.

All this indicates, to me that something is wrong. I believe that we should all be concerned and try to do what we can to get off this track to a bland white hell.

I want to do something in this society that will make a difference and help. I hope that by sharing my art I can help to challenge people's preconceived notions and prejudices by opening their eyes to the beauty, wonder and excitement I see in this world.

If you are interested in more information or purchasing Eban Lehrer's work, write to him at P.O. Box 39703, Los Angeles, CA 90039

She-wolf (1992)

Triad (1992)

Metamorphosis (1993)

Feminine Vortex (1991)

Purple Veils, 1992 —slashed while on display in restaurant.

Censored . . . *by Eban Lehrer*

As I write this, I see a painting out of the corner of my eye. This painting has been slashed from top to bottom. Seems somebody had a violent reaction to what they saw. This painting was vandalized in a restaurant in a major hotel in Los Angeles. (Supposedly liberal L. A.).

This is not the first time that somebody has objected to my imagery, but, this is the first time that I have ever had a piece of work (and by extension, myself) violently attacked.

I paint in this restaurant every Sunday during the brunch to add to the ambience. When I first started painting there I wanted to paint what I would usually paint in my studio. And that requires a nude model. The restaurant didn't think a nude model would add to their ambience.

So, I painted other things (abstracts, still lifes, etc.). I brought in finished pictures to leave there to be exhibited. It was one of those that was defaced. Because of this I will no longer leave any painting at the restaurant that may offend anyone.

The picture that was slashed is not obscene (I consider violence to be obscene). It is a creature comprised of portions of the female anatomy (eyes, breasts and genitalia).

The violent nature of the attack on this painting exemplifies the whole reason behind my painting what I paint.

This is not the first time I have run into problems. Once, the night after I had just installed a show in another restaurant,

I was called by the owner and told he had taken some of my paintings down. He said that a few people had complained and asked that I replace the 'offensive ' pictures with 'non-offensive' ones.

These 'offensive' pictures were surreal abstractions of vulvas. (I guess food and what some people think are representations of sexuality do not mix).

I've also been told by a gallery owner that some of my art is too visceral. Specifically, he was referring to paintings of creatures that look like they are comprised of portions of the female anatomy. This same person has shown other works of mine (colorful portraits). Now, I thought the whole idea behind art was to be visceral and evoke a strong reaction. Oh well, silly me, I guess we all want to look at pretty pictures of clowns and dogs playing poker.

There have been many other instances where I have been told by galleries, restaurants and even coffeehouses that my work is tremendous but they are afraid to show it for fear of offending someone.

As a result of all this, I now spend some of my time thinking about how to make art that I like that is 'acceptable'. And I've learned that if you spend too much of your time thinking and trying to figure things out, instead of painting from the gut, something usually gets lost in the translation. Sad, isn't it?

BREAKING THE CHAINS OF SELF-CENSORSHIP

John Rousso

In 1968 at the age of eighteen, I wrote a poem about love, censorship and religion. It was probably an outcry for help in understanding what was happening in my life at the time and what was expected of me in the future. We've all had our broken hearts but what was unusual, I think now in retrospect, was my dissatisfaction with the church and censorship.

My favorite saint was Saint Christopher, the patron saint of travelers. The Catholic church has commemorative days for each saint. One day "they" decided to remove Saint Christopher "Patron Saint of Travelers" and put in someone else who I never heard of. I was outraged. Christopher was a saint that even non-Catholics knew. My faith in the church quickly dwindled from that point, but I still wear my Saint Christopher medal.

Woodstock hadn't happened as of yet so the censors were still employing their puritanical ways on people, and my mind was still in tumult over what a boy of eighteen was supposed to be like.

Time passes. As the years went by I never forgot that poem and the censors of the church who always seemed to keep up with their medieval thinking. The problem with this paradine is the damage it does to an impressionable mind. One starts to second guess his or her abilities, identity, purpose and well being. Dress codes, fashions, fads cliques, gangs, teachers and authoritative figures all play a role in molding your mind.

When I was in art school a friend gave me a poem by Morris L. West "The Shoes of the Fisherman." One section, in particular, spoke to me:

"It cost so much to be a free human being that there are very few who have the enlightenment or the courage to pay the price. One has to abandon altogether the search for security and reach out to the risk of living with both arms."

Security was so drilled into us that imagination and interpretation had no room to breathe. What does it all mean? Simple, the worst imposed censorship of all, is self-censorship.

All our teachings or misteachings have to be unrolled, dissected, mulched and uningested.

Time passes. Security grows, maybe not in a material sense but from within. Until this happens self-censorship remains in control destroying our abilities, our identity. In the series "The Requiem" (selected portions illustrating this essay) the objective was to push the button on people's fears and misteachings; to destroy controlled censorship or self-imposed censorship; to awaken our feelings, our sexuality, our desires and throw our arms around ourselves and say "Yes" I have security. We must step into the unknown or dark side of our hidden desires to enhance our pleasure and/or pain which collectively comprises our sexuality, our being, our identity.

My days of censorship by galleries or jurored shows are past. The artist in finding him or herself must plunge on because without artists, the masses will transform into Saint Christopher and lose their day.

The art of Eban Lehrer and John Rousso were displayed at the 3rd Annual Sensual & Erotic Art Exhibition held in Las Vegas in August. For further information contact The Lifestyles Organization - 2641 W. La Palma, Suite A, Anaheim, CA 92801. Phone: 714-821-9953

Control copyright © 1992

Desire © 1992 *(top) and* Reparation © 1992 *(bottom)*

THE 'VELOPES

Davo

In this vast artistic wasteland of the United States where only the mediocre artist survives, and true artistic expression is extinguished daily by the need to eke out a living, long-time artists Terry Davis and Wayne Hitchcock continue to create a controversial art form outside the mainstream of regional galleries and corporate controlled media. Their avenue of expression is the lowly, white business envelope, and their platform is the U.S. mail.

What makes their art controversial are the images they create on the outside of the envelopes and the suppression they receive from, of all places, the United States Postal Service. These envelopes, or 'Velopes, as they are known, are bizarre, comic, political and oftentimes erotic depictions of free-wheeling, unbridled creativity. Drawn from very personal perspectives, the 'Velope' have evolved over the course of 15 years from a simple, decorative device to provide greater visibility and thus guarantee delivery, to a means of expressing the inexpressible. From an empty blank space that was dying to be adorned with artistic embellishments, the envelopes became the 'Velopes, the creation of a new "thing". They progressed into a place to put 'personal' art on display and to communicate beyond the mere words inside. As time

went on, they expanded into a movable gallery of flowing art reflecting illustrated moments of imaginary time from the lives of two artists communicating in their own special way. They also serve as a release from the frustration of having no forum for art of a hazardous nature. They are a place to put anything at all . . . a cartoon, a portrait, a wish, a dream, a fear, a woman without clothes.

After all, who is going to see them and who really cares? And so any topic could be addressed, from homophobia and the aids epidemic to the toxic destruction of the environment and the never-ending carnage of animals squashed along the highway. From glimpses into the artists' personal lives of folly to nose-picking motorists, no subject is out of bounds. No idea is forbidden. And then there is sex . . . a device long used as an attention grabber in every day advertising, and sure to capture the individual notice of any bleary-eyed mail carrier.

And why not? As anyone who has ever known an artist can tell you, sex, either real or imagined, plays a large role in artists' lives, and the 'Velopes art like all art, are expressions of those lives. To omit or deny sex would be only a shadow of the truth rather than a genuine reflection. So that in creating a particular 'Velope, if the portrayal of a nude man or woman seems appropriate, as it has throughout arts' long history, then it is rendered as such, without any thought of censorship. Freedom to use any image in the pursuit of artistic expression is analogous to the freedom to use any medium or technique. In fact, the 'Velopes themselves are one continuous experiment using all the creative elements that the artist can conjure up, without knowing what the end result will be. It is here that the real danger exists. When the artists let go of the "known" and delve into the "unknown". Not because he uses images that may be judged salacious or deviant by an emasculated postal official.

Yet the spirit of playfulness and freedom that naturally arises out of creative activity is out of step with the impersonal code of military toughness used by the Post Office in deciding which art to deliver and which art to destroy. A number of the erotic 'Velopes have been intercepted and delayed, only to turn up 'covered' in a plain brown wrapper, with a note from the local postal official urging the recipient to urge the (unsigned) sender to discontinue the practice of decorating envelopes with subject matter deemed "objectionable" (by someone), and threatening to have further such envelopes sent to the Dead Letter Office for proper disposal. Indeed, some 'Velopes were never delivered and are assumed to have been destroyed.

After some investigation it was learned that the Postal Service will not deliver what it doesn't want to deliver and covers itself with various statues, in this case postal regulation 123.45d — Lewd or filthy matter (18 usc 1461,1463) "Obscene, lewd, lascivious or filthy publications or writings, or mail containing information concerning where, how, or from whom such matter may be obtained, and matter that is otherwise mailable but has on it's wrapper or envelope any indecent, lewd, lascivious or obscene writing or printing. *Any mail containing any filthy, vile, or indecent thing.*"

When it comes to art traveling through the mail, the question is, what is a filthy, vile or indecent thing? In this case it is the human body, its parts and its functions. In an attempt to establish a new art arena for the expression of unrestricted artistic freedom, which is rarely found elsewhere in today's insular culture, two

artists have run afoul of another of society's humorless guard dogs. And despite the fact that their art is unknown and unseen by all but a few close friends, an occasional politician and miscellaneous postal workers, they continue to wage a small battle against the gluttonous conformity and complacency that has so much of American culture in its authoritarian grip.

Chances are the 'Velopes will never be shown in any of the timid, staid galleries in Yourtown, U.S.A. Their only public appearance came for two short weeks in the winter of 1991. 100 'Velopes were shown at the final show of the only art gallery in New London, Connecticut, which closed shortly thereafter . Although notified well in advance, no local reporters came to review the show, and without the press coverage, the show technically never happened.

The world is full of groveling artists willing to stay away from unpopular themes in order to enjoy the prestige of having their work shown in today's exclusive galleries. Indeed, they have little choice if they hope to curry the favor of those in power, upon whom their reputations and lifestyles depend . Yet however talented they are by society's standards, they have no right to call themselves artists. That distinction was lost the moment they chose to ignore their own inner voice in preference to the dictates of the public opinion. Perhaps there is some comfort in knowing that there are at least two artists today who have remained true to themselves and prefer to make art in their own way.

THROUGH THE BACK DOOR

James Healy

Back in the 1980s artists in America and abroad were scrambling around and compromising themselves for the chance to show their art in venues; galleries that supposedly were the new spaces for the so-called post-modern avant garde, run by funds granted to them by the NEA and others who wanted to bake their cake and eat it too. I was living in the southwest corner of the nation and said fuck that shit. There was no way in hell that I was going to buckle under to the pressure of a system that was so screwed up. I wasn't about to take the easy route and become another puppet on the strings of the local and national fund raisers hands.

By happenstance, at this time **Rita Dean** was born. While finishing a series of erotic paintings that were going to show in an upcoming exhibit, this gorgeous creature walked by. Her name happened to be **RITA**. It was then I decided if a woman signed my

paintings they might be more desirable. The self-censorship seemed to be a way to manipulate the situation to my benefit. But was all of this necessary? You be the judge.

At the time an exhibit director approached me about being in a show. I was thrilled until a friend told me another artist had been rejected because his work was too explicit. I submitted some of my work under my own name; other *more erotic* work under the name Rita Dean (Dean being my middle name).

Two weeks later the work under my name was rejected as being too bold. That same day the exhibitor called, wanting to contact "Rita Dean" as he wanted to make *her* work the centerpiece of the exhibit. He was intrigued there was a woman who wasn't afraid to show her sexual side. I played my cards all the way to the show's opening. When the show opened the director was freaking out because he wanted to meet Rita

Teenagers, Tequilla, and Tijuana

When the crowds left

Dean. I told him then what I'd done, yet he refused to believe me and eventually asked me to leave.

The following day he called to apologize and requested that I provide another series . . . *under the name of Rita Dean*. This time I politely refused.

But I wasn't about to let the myth die; not in the context of the times we were living. As I became more successful I needed more room to exhibit my work. Ironically I procured a store front position between two gun shops. Now this space was much larger than my previous one, so I was able to add a subversive bookstore in the front of the gallery.

This was ideal to the **Rita Dean** philosophy; uncensored literature between two gun shops was better

than fantasy. What could be more dangerous than books and guns next door to each other? The gallery was renamed the **Rita Dean Gallery**. The only way to keep the space interesting was to exhibit the work the so-called alternative, avant garde, post modern, and GOD-fearing NEA diplomats wouldn't touch. That meant *anything* that had to do with SEX, DEATH, RELIGION, and POLITICS. The first exhibit I sponsored was the 1st Annual Erotica Exhibit "Caught Looking," which was so well received that I decided it would become an annual event since there are so many sexual hang-ups out there in our civilized society.

The gallery evolved as a place to exhibit what everyone else censored. Thus **Rita Dean** could become fully operational through everyone else's neglect with their own vehicles. It's like taking parts from one vehicle to make another one run; instead of running down to the parts department I salvaged what everyone else had disregarded as junk.

And please remember what ever doesn't kill you can only make you stronger.

The Rita Dean Gallery is located at 544 Sixth Ave., San Diego, CA. 92101; phone (619)338-8153. Upcoming exhibits include

November: International Aids Portrait Show
December: Peter Spaans Marble Hill Project
January: Paintings of the Homeless
February: Charles Gatewood/Michael Yamamoto photographs

Sexual Interpretations

ON OUR BACKS GETS KICKED IN THE ASS

On our Backs is a magazine that, according to former-editor Marcy Scheiner, "publishes depictions of explicit lesbian sexuality." You won't find it at major chains because of its sexual explicitness and Scheiner says some women's bookstores refuse to stock it because they feel it's anti-feminist.

On Our Backs worst brush with censorship, however, came when they decided to go glossy. Their San Francisco printer did not have the capability at the time, so they shopped in the midwest (where prices are best). Actually, they were solicited by Dimension Graphics a printer in Kansas. The magazine went with Dimension Graphics "because they'd shown a lack of homophobia," says Scheiner, "by printing explicit heterosexual porn." To be on the safe side, however, their art director "grilled the sales rep about what they would and would not print and was assured that even penetration would not be a problem."

The first issue went smoothly. With the next issue the honeymoon ended.

With all material at the printers *On Our Back* received a call from Dimension Graphics that two photos in a pictorial of Aminta had crossed the line. Scheiner considers the spread to be "the most soft-core pictorial in the

issue. She was playing with a dildo for godsakes! But it was a *black* dildo."

The concern was not only a possible delay in publication, but the very real possibility the printer might destroy original material: "What was different now was that the entire contents of the magazine — original photos, editorial copy, ads — was in the hands of a bunch of unknown white heterosexual men in Kansas. For all we knew, if we didn't cooperate with them we might never see any of it again — a major loss for us as well as for our contributors," Scheiner relates.

The staff relented and sent new material to replace what had offended the printer. Dimension Graphics wasn't through, though. A week later they called *On Our Backs*, this time objecting to Annie Sprinkle's photos "of a woman licking pussy through saran wrap." According to Scheiner, "These photos are not only hot, but they are essential educational tools. They represent a very rare phenomenon: graphic portrayals of how lesbians can protect themselves from sexually transmitted diseases." These, too, were replaced.

With the magazine finally printed and shipped, Scheiner confronted Dimension Graphics to determine whether the offending art violated Kansas law or just the printer's sensibilities. She relates her conversation: "I phoned the printer and inquired as to which laws I should be aware of in planning future

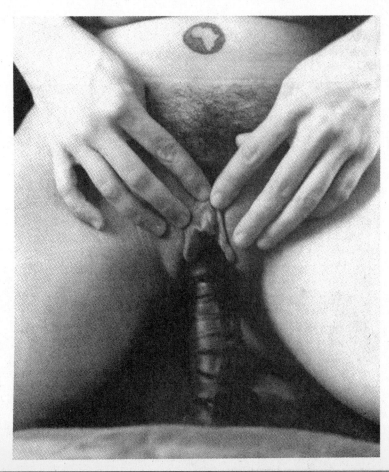

issues of *On Our Backs*. He ran a rap about penetration, explicit or implied. Yes, I said, we understand, but exactly which law does this fall under? He unabashedly informed me that his policy had nothing whatever to do with the law, that it was a 'corporate decision.' 'This is where we draw the line. These are our personal mores.'"

While arguably printers can reject any material they find objectionable (there are no laws to protect the client even *after* contracts have been signed), the abuse of power of the printer here was particularly insidious. Scheiner feels: "By actively soliciting business from publishers of sexual materials, then asking them to tone down their work Dimension Graphics is employing tactics alarm-ingly similar to those used by the anti-abortion movement, who pose as 'abortion counselors' and then show vulnerable pregnant women grisly films of aborted fetuses."

On Our Backs found a new printer, but an invaluable lesson was learned the hard way. We've printed the offending photos so you can see what caused the ruckus.

---

*Readers who want to question Dimension Graphics (they refused to answer our questions) can contact them at 13915 West 107th, Lenexa, KS 66215. If you want more information regarding **On Our Backs**, they can be reached at 526 Castro St., San Francisco, CA 94114.*

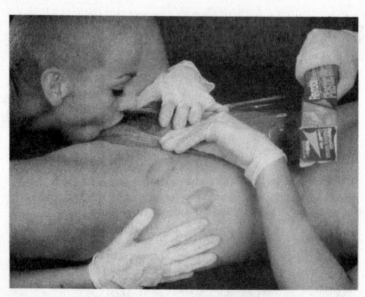

photo by Annie Sprinkle

Drawing Upon the Imagination
THE ART OF
CLIVE BARKER

Lisa Petrucci

Like so many projects that Clive Barker has had a hand in to date, it's to be expected that his first solo exhibition of paintings and drawings (at Bess Cutler Gallery, 379 West Broadway, New York, NY 10012 — March 19 through April 24, 1993) was a journey into a deeply personal side of this master of horror and fantasy.

If you didn't already know, Clive Barker makes art. Real art. He's been doing it for most of his life, and the exhibition focuses on the past twenty years of his production. Probably the most readily available place to get a glimpse of his art previously has been in special edition books and novels that Clive has illustrated himself (*Books of Blood Volumes I-VI, The Great and Secret*

Show, Weaveworld, and most recently *The Thief of Always* — a delightfully morbid fairy tale for children of all ages.) There are also entire books written about Clive's art: the *Clive Barker Illustrator* which gives an excellent overview of his art, chock full of pictures and texts, *Pandemonium*, and *Shadows in Eden*, besides the numerous fanzines devoted to the world of Barker.

Perhaps you'd expect to see countless gory, grim images plastering the walls, but not so. The horrific element is presented minimally at best. Like many of his earlier books and films (the *Books of Blood* and *Hellraiser* come to mind), a few of the paintings tap into the visually macabre and revel in detailed, fleshy representations of humans and monsters pushing the limits of their physicality and psyche. Bosch and Bruegel would feel at home amidst the psycho-sex landscapes Clive manufactured for his *Books of Blood* paintings. Lovingly rendered grotesqueries; a group portrait of humans and creatures mingling around a snapshot photo of their creator; in another, Marilyn Monroe smiles while she is surrounded by rows of tiny dancing skulls and floating eyeballs, her upswept dress fringed with snarling fangs and poor Mickey Mouse cries tears of blood from empty sockets. And then another features a crazed, laughing man who appears to be in the throes of ecstacy as his skin is ripped away and hypodermic needles pierce into his exposed brain. The paintings from this series are truly magnificent and show off Clive's technical ability to the max.

On the other hand, the more recent paintings come from a more spiritual tradition, closer to that of the Symbolists and Expressionists. He doesn't have to bombast the senses anymore. These tend to be inspired from mythology and his

Clive Barker "Carna (Sketch)
The Thief of Always" 1992

deepest imagination. Often the subjects of Clive's work — male, female, creature — appear to be going through a state of self-imposed change and fluxuation. Genders and bodies merge into newly discovered state of being. Transformation is at the heart of his writing and artmaking, and these ideas are explored on many levels in this exhibition. Sexuality is celebrated and subverted — in relation to the self and a realm of other possibilities.

In the large triptych oil painting "Axis — Primal Goddess, The Christ Condition Modern Man" (1993), three large archetypal figures solidly fixed in a stark, ochre landscape. A voluptuous earth-mother, bursting at the seams with life, claws her way across the horizon while a heroic central figure supports a lifeless, bloody body across his back. This unholy silhouette mocks a crucifix. Below this pair is being protected by a beastlike demon. The final canvas depicts a haunting image of a solitary man who is contained within a roach-encrusted armor. These ambitious canvases convince me that Clive can paint; I'm remained of Max Beckman's large oils when confronted by this apocalyptic trio.

A walk around the gallery can become an exercise in deciphering Clive's personal obsessions and his reaction to interior and exterior stimulation. Many of the pictures are surprisingly revealing (his sexual preference screams out loud and strong!) Although the subconscious remains his foremost tool and inspiration, it is clearly evident that he is familiar with other artists, particularly favoring the movements of the late nineteenth and early twentieth centuries. There is a bit of the previously mentioned Symbolism and Expressionism and also some Surrealism thrown in, but Clive constantly reinvents and twists their icongraphy to suit his journey into the "fantasitque."

His drawings run the gamut stylistically. Some are academically rendered figures and studies executed in a loose linear way, other are bolder and heavy — but always his markmaking is economical and simple. At one point he uses ballpoint pen or fineline marker to doodle and crosshatch, other times he switches over to sumi brush and ink (which he has a

Clive Barker **Books of Blood, Vol. IV** *1986*

real knack for). These latter works are strongly influenced by Oriental graphics, especially the Japanese manga-scrolls and books which were the predecessor of the modern comic book.

Throughout his career, Clive's sketches have served as notes for his other projects. He has kept the documentation of his ideas, and designs for theater productions and films are amongst the more familiar imagery in the exhibition. What a treat to see the original concept drawings for the Cenobites in *Hellraiser*! It's pretty fascinating how these translated to film. His ink portraits of the monsters are elegant and noble — almost classical in their treatment. The metamorphos is to the character we know as Pinhead is remarkable. With these designs Clive created a new type of monster — based on his own interest in sadomasochism and an understanding of the psychology of desire. His use of S+M fashion and ideology many have even contributed to the exposure of piercing and body modification to our subculture during the eighties.

Barker's choice of pen, ink and brush places him somewhere outside of most current contemporary art, and somewhere between traditional artmaking and more graphically oriented work. His drawings are at ease in the gallery space and the printed page. Clive, like so many of the more interesting artists steadily gaining recognition outside of the underground (R. Williams, R. Crumb, C. Burns, G. Panter, etc.), is finally having the opportunity to get his work dispersed in the public domain. May popular culture live long, hard and strong!

Clive Barker **Books of Blood, Vol. I** 1985

Clive Barker will be having an exhibition at the Bess Cutler Gallery annex in Los Angeles this fall. For further information on the show and original art please contact the gallery at 212-219-1577. Lisa Petrucci is a curator at the Bess Cutler Gallery and freelance writer.

Clive Barker **Books of Blood, Vol. III** 1985

Clive Barker "The Muser" 1993 Ink on paper 24 x 18"

Clive Barker "Prisoner" 1981 Ink on paper 8 x 11 1/2

Clive Barker "Seated Man" 1989 Oil on Canvas 60 x 48"

Those Happy 1950s

Chelsea Quinn Yarbro

Last winter while I was at one of those compulsory holiday gatherings, I happened to hear one of the guests remarking that the last really happy times the country had had was the 1950s, and that everything since then had been a tragic fall from grace. In his memories, the 50s were secure, reliable, and pleasant, filled with the rosy glow of nostalgia and status quo. He admitted he wanted a return to that kind of society, where you knew how things were supposed to be. What was astonishing to me was that he was saying here, in my home town, Berkeley, California, a place where the 50s were anything but happy.

For me, and for a lot of the people I grew up with, the 50s was a time of witch-hunting, Red-baiting, bomb-shelters, and condemnation by innuendo.

It is easy for most of the USA to look at the national paranoia now as a kind of isolationistic Eden, a withdrawal from the international scene at the close of World War II; most of the country did not get caught up in the Red scare directly, at least no more directly than what they heard on the evening news, when much of the population would mutter that Edward R. Murrow was going a little too far to take after Joe McCarthy the way he did — after all, all Tail-Gunner Joe was trying to do was get the Commies out of the country, and that was a good thing for everyone: J. Edgar Hoover said so. So what if some people lost their jobs, or were punished for refusing to name their friends and associates who might have said or done something at one time or another to support a movement or a cause thought to have links to Communism? They probably deserved what happened to them.

My own recollections of this time begin with an argument I overheard between my parents early in 1952, after the Rosenbergs were sentenced but before their execution; I was nine and in fourth grade; it was spring. The argument was about my father's oldest brother and his wife, who lived in Mendocino County, and who were under investigation for subversive activities. My uncle had done time in San Quentin in the 30s for union organizing with loggers and mill workers, making him clearly a dangerous fellow. His wife was of Russian-Jewish heritage and came originally from New York where she had been a professional translator specializing in Eastern European languages. Very suspicious, as well. My parents were arguing about taking in my two cousins if their parents were put on trial and/or sent to prison. My father, being self-employed, was prepared to do this for his brother. But my mother, who taught art history at Cal, was not, for fear of losing her job, and possibly being required to testify against her in-laws, which she did not want to do. She was also afraid that if we took in my cousins, the government would make life very hard for all of us. The whole question remained up in the air for several months.

A few weeks after this overheard disagreement, I was walking home from school down Terrace Walk, the most direct route home from the school. I became aware I was being followed by a man in a dark business suit, which troubled me; there had been a recent case of a man exposing himself to girls on the playground, and so everyone was jumpy. Men in business suits were not often encountered on Terrace Walk at three in the afternoon. Knowing things were pretty dicey at home, I said nothing, not wanting to cause more difficulties for my parents. But when it happened again, I did as we had been instructed to do — I told my teacher, an elderly maiden lady of timorous nature named Miss Hoffman, who took the story to the Principal.

Two days later I was called to the Principal's office, I thought to give a full report on the man who was following me; instead I was issued a stern warning by the Principal that the men following me were from the FBI and they were doing an important job protecting our country from dangerous people. Precisely what I had to do with these dangerous people I did not know, nor was I told, except that the FBI was following me in order to catch them. However, Miss Hoffman heard all this, and from that day until school let out in June, life in the fourth grade was wretched for me; she was convinced I was a dangerous influence on the class, filled with unAmerican ideas. She made it plain that she believed I was clearly being used by my parents to help them do bad-but-unspecified

things, and the fact that I was not ashamed of these things made it worse. Of course, I never had a clue what these bad things might be, except that they were somehow linked to Uncle Oscar and Aunt Beatrice, and had something to do with my bribing boys to take books out of the boys' side of the library for me, because that's where all the good books were.

About this time my mother cut back her teaching schedule, limiting herself to her favorites, the French Impressionists, and her classload from six to three. She said she wanted to spend more time with her family. While that might have been a factor, the pressure her decision took off her probably had more to do with it.

Why should an art historian worry about being fired under these circumstances? Because it had already happened to people we knew: one man, a professor of botany, had been asked to resign from the university because he had been in correspondence with Russian botanists. Never mind that their researches were in similar areas of agricultural interests, it was thought to be too dangerous to let a man with so much Soviet influence in his thinking to be permitted to reach those tender, suggestible minds of undergrads who might be contaminated by theories on plant growth. His wife was not allowed to volunteer at her local polling place or during voter registration drives, because she might exercise undue influence on those voting or registering to vote. Eventually the professor became a partner in a large commercial nursery in the Salinas Valley, and moved his family there.

Another family who had struggled to keep in contact with relatives in the Soviet Union — a patriotic thing to do in World War II — suddenly found that no one would give a

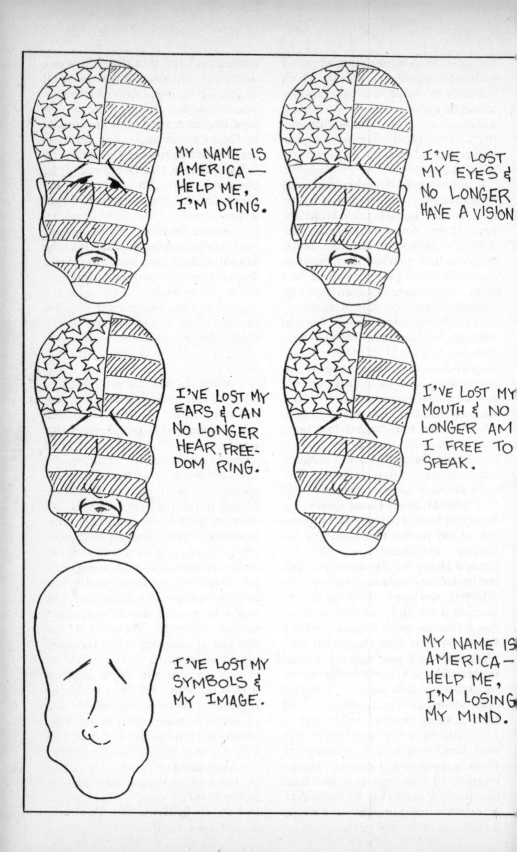

commission to an architect who had such questionable connections; the marriage broke up and the man left the area. I learned later from his son who was my classmate in high school that his father had committed suicide a few years before.

Whatever it was the FBI thought I was doing, apparently they decided I wasn't, because after about two more weeks of this nerve-wracking surveillance, it stopped. When I finally got up enough courage to ask the Principal, he said that we were very lucky that nothing was discovered. Whatever that means, it was all the explanation I was given at the time, although later I was told that girls carrying books on dinosaurs and astronomy, certainly not what any girl would want to know about, was often thought to be a courier, with messages concealed in big books. At least that was the wisdom at the time.

Who did they think I was carrying messages for, and to what purpose? And what nefarious foreign spy would use a nine-year-old girl to carry hidden messages from grammar school five blocks to home? Who did they think my connection was? One of the other children? A teacher? The librarian, who was displeased at my bribery of male classmates in any case? One of the cafeteria workers? Perhaps I was meeting a spy and exchanging envelopes and packages somewhere on the two-block stretch of Terrace Walk? Certainly in as suspect a place as Berkeley, the Communists were not so utterly desperate for help that they needed to use a child to carry messages for them?

Looking at it now, it all seems a little silly, ridiculously over-blown; witch-hunting is such a quaint phrase, bringing to mind ignorant peasants with pitchforks and torches. But everyone who spoke out against this suppression at the time was made to pay the price for questioning the political dogma of the happy 50s. Before the hysteria was over, more than ten families my family knew personally had lost their employment and their general standing in the community, though none of them were ever actually accused of a crime in any court. Eventually a paralyzing trepidation settled over the community, permeating more than the curriculum at Cal.

What this kind of insidious fear does to such things as the First Amendment cannot be underestimated. People today are beginning to realize the horrible impact the HUAC (House UnAmerican Activities Committee) had on the entertainment industry, but the earlier terrorization of teachers has largely been overlooked. During the 50s, teachers were afraid to take on subjects that might be considered subversive, and were reported to the FBI by students who feared that they had been given unAmerican information in their standard lectures. There was also the whole mess about loyalty oaths: certain universities and colleges required teachers to sign a loyalty oath to the USA as a condition of employment. Luckily this was vigorously opposed and eventually overruled, but not until a number of highly qualified teachers had lost their jobs and sacrificed a large part of their academic credibility to the whispering campaign that followed such resistance.

My aunt and uncle were never actually charged with Un-American activities, largely because there was nothing to charge them with, aside from being politically leftist, but they were harassed by the FBI for a period of fifteen years.

And to this day, I am uneasy on Terrace Walk.

THE MISSING DEMAND IN THE GAY AGENDA

Michael Medved

In all the nearly six hours of speeches at the recent gay and lesbian march on Washington, and in all the countless manifestos generally associated with today's powerful push for homosexual rights, there is one demand, one agenda item, that has been conspicuous by its absence.

To the best of my knowledge, no significant leader of this movement has suggested that we implement "affirmative action" for homosexuals.

It seems fair to ask why not.

The drive for gay rights is repeatedly compared to previous civil rights campaigns for African-Americans, Latinos, women and others. All of those previous movements, however, have called for affirmative action — or, on occasion, outright quotas — as a key precondition for progress.

With gays currently portrayed as American's latest disadvantaged minority, why shouldn't the same strategy be applied to them?

The two part answer to this question demonstrates why it is so terribly misleading to describe the movement for gay rights as just one more campaign for equal justice.

The first obstacle in establishing any quota program for gays and lesbians is that this segment of the population is so notoriously hard to count.

The controversy concerning recent studies that show homosexuals as 1% of American adults, rather than the 10% that gay activists claim, only highlights the difficulties in reaching consensus on accurate numbers.

The problems in this process would be enough to drive any bureaucratic bean counter around the bend. What percentage of a given profession would have to be openly homosexual before that elite could satisfy authorities that gay people had been granted equality of opportunity? Who would qualify as "gay", anyway? What about a suburban father and husband who had a brief homosexual affair five years ago? Could you count him as gay for affirmative action purposes?

But beyond the obvious problems in enumerating who is gay and who is not for the purposes of governmental score-keeping, there is another powerful reason that homosexual activists aren't interested in establishing some quota system based on sexual orientation.

In many crucial areas traditionally targeted by affirmative action programs, gays are already over-represented — and they know it.

In fact, one of the major themes that emerged in the Washington march (which I attended as a spectator) involved an unmistakable note of gay triumphalism — unabashed pride in the many positions of influence and authority now occupied by homosexuals.

Andrew Kopkind, for instance, in his much discussed article "The Gay Moment" in The Nation declared: "There would hardly be modern art, literature or philosophy without gay sensibility . . . Broadway is bursting with gay plays, big book awards go to gay authors

. . . 'Queer theory'— also known as lesbian and gay studies — is explored by scholars and students at hundreds of colleges . . . There are hundreds of new organizations formed by gays in professions (journalism, law, medicine, psychotherapy, teaching) . . . The ascension of gay people to positions of authority in key sectors of society has made a huge difference in the weather."

Kopkind and his colleagues seem oblivious to the glaring contradiction in their messages. On the one hand, they boast of the disproportionate influence of the gay community on our culture and our society, and on the other they continue to claim the status of a disadvantaged minority.

This contradiction is reenforced by some of the most recent studies of the gay male population. For instance, last month's unusually thorough survey by the Battelle Research Centers which attracted so much media attention, showed that homosexual experience is 40 times more common among those who hold college degrees than among those who never completed high school, and that exclusive gay orientation is similarly skewed in the direction of the more educated respondents.

Even more striking, are the numbers gathered by Simmons Market

Research concerning the 200,000 readers of *The Advocate*, the nation's leading gay magazine. Those readers boast an average annual income of $62,000 — nearly twice the national average. They are also more than twice as likely to own a CD player, and 20 times more likely to have vacationed abroad in the last three years.

While gays can certainly be found in every walk of life and in all economic strata, statistics suggest that as a group they occupy a relatively privileged position in society. No one can deny the existence of gay janitors and welfare recipients, but the homosexual population is unquestionably concentrated in the professions, the arts, academia, the media and other influential elites.

If any strictly enforced quota system were applied to these fields, based upon percentages of sexual orientation in the general population, it would surely hurt, rather than help, the gay community.

In discussing this question with one of my gay colleagues, he freely acknowledged that homosexuals represent a disproportionately prosperous sub-group within the society, and he believes that a process of self-selection helps to explain the situation. According to his reasoning, the more educated, artistic and sophisticated you happen to be, the less there is that you will succumb to homophobic attitudes — and therefore you will be more likely to recognize and accept your own gay impulses. This argument, however, would be anathema to most gay activists —because it posits an uncomfortable element of volition, of informed choice, when it comes to defining sexual orientation.

However one explains the remarkable achievements of a community that is so relatively small (no matter whose numbers you accept), the prestige and prosperity of so many homosexuals highlights the way that their current push for "equal justice" is fundamentally different from other civil rights struggles of recent years.

The gay rights agenda includes no affirmative action demands because that agenda is not focused on economic opportunity, or access to the establishment. It concentrates, rather, on winning acceptance and respect for those who choose to live their lives openly as homosexuals. The most pressing demands involve a change in private attitudes rather than an increase in practical opportunities.

The fact that the gay rights movement is fundamentally and profoundly different from previous advocacy campaigns by other embattled minorities doesn't necessarily make its aims invalid. But it does suggest that homosexual activists confuse public discourse and undermine their own credibility when they try to downplay the unique and unprecedented nature of the controversial mass movement they have launched.

Michael Medved is co-host of **Sneak Previews** *on PBS-TV and film critic for the* **New York Post**. *He is also the author of* **Hollywood vs. America** *and six other non-fiction books*

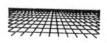

T UE PERVERSIO

Stan Leventhal

One of the more perverse aspects of the increasing mainstream media coverage of queer culture and politics is the huge gap between reality and perception. As more independently distributed books and films illuminate all of the shadowy realms of life as we know it, the commercial media — and its henchpersons — still attempt to obscure the cold hard truths. Lies and misinformation not only get a hearing, but become recycled by journalists and broadcasters who are too lazy or ignorant to get the facts.

In the guise of concern and compassion, Michael Medved writes about affirmative action and the gay community, and one can only wonder why this writer is begging an argument. To make a big deal of a non-issue is surely an attention-grabbing device that only a desperate, ill-advised reporter would attempt. But it does nothing to clarify the real problems facing mainstream America, only adds to its rampant homophobia.

It is unfortunate that with all of the accurate information available regarding the queer people of America, most people's ideas and opinions are shaped by media bias. And many believe that what they are being told is the truth, so they are not motivated to look any further, dig any deeper. It is apparent that Medved knows nothing about gay culture or the queer community, nor does he seem to have much awareness of minority cultures in general. For him to lump together all of America's minorities, and simplistically ignore the vast differences in their problems and goals, calls into question not only his ability, but the editor and publisher who provide his forum.

The reason why affirmative action is not of concern to gays is because many of us are invisible. Most African-Americans and other people of color do not have that option. Sad that Medved cannot see this distinction, nor the complications which differentiate the needs of lesbians and gay men. Moreover, his claim that there is no need for a gay liberation movement because some gay people have attained positions of power in certain professions, obscures the fact that gays who have made significant contributions in the arts are only a small percentage of the overall gay population and mostly male; that the gays who become prominent politically only have as much clout as the media allows; and that most gay people lead ordinary lives and constantly have problems with their jobs, apartments and homes, with the general mood of homophobia which permeates all areas of American life. Because Medved can point to a few successful gay people does not mean that we don't have major problems that need to be solved.

I wonder if Medved has ever read anything by Randy Shilts, Lillian Faderman, Sarah Schulman, Harlan Greene, Jewelle Gomez, Martin Duberman, Randall Kenan, Michael Nava or Dorothy Allison? Or if he's ever talked to any openly gay people? The difference between Medved and a writer with principles is that those who know nothing about nuclear reactors, for example, don't expect to see their opinions on them in print. He, however, has no trouble broadcasting his ignorance, obviously unconcerned with just how much damage more media misinformation can engender. If he had any integrity he would stick to writing about Schwarzenegger and Stallone movies, a job which requires very little in the way of truth or knowledge.

Stan Leventhal is the author of numerous books including Mountain Climbing in Sheridan Square, A Herd of Tiny Elephants and Candy Holidays

THE POTSHOT HEARD 'ROUND THE WORLD

Wayne Jebian

"Brownie Mary" Rathbun is a local hero, an ex-pot dealer turned angel of mercy. She has worked in San Francisco for the past 9 years as an AIDS volunteer, delivering free marijuana brownies to AIDS patients until her arrest on July 21, 1992. Charged with possession of 2 1/2 pounds of pot, Mary Rathbun at 69 years of age faced the possibility of spending the remainder of her natural life in prison. The AIDS patients to whom she delivered her wares, as well as most of the population of San Francisco, stood behind her. The San Francisco board of Supervisors declared August 25th to be "Brownie Mary Day" in Rathbun's honor, making her a symbol of the ongoing struggle for medical marijuana. On December 15th, 1992, the Sonoma County District Attorney dropped the charges against her, giving up the case against this popular, sympathetic figure.

Widely recommended by oncologists for its ability to alleviate nausea suffered by chemotherapy patients, marijuana has recently been used by an increasing number of people suffering from AIDS. The head of the AIDS program at San Francisco General Hospital recommends that marijuana be made available to these patients and the California Medical Association concurs. The value of medical marijuana is so widely recognized in the San Francisco area that in November, 1991 79.5% of San Francisco voters passed a measure known as proposition P, a local ordinance that legalizes prescription pot. In the 1992 election, two more California counties, Santa Cruz and Marin, passed medical marijuana bills of their own, even though marijuana is still banned altogether under Federal Law. "Brownie Mary" Rathbun was arrested outside San Francisco city limits, however, and was treated by local authorities as a common criminal.

Rathbun predicted that a court victory for her would be "a shot heard round the world" for medical marijuana, but she may have spoken too soon. In most areas of the United States, California's "marijuana revolution" has been met with widespread indifference. Very few East Coast newspapers and virtually no national publications consider such developments newsworthy.

In recent years, a great deal of evidence has emerged that marijuana is an extremely useful substance, not only to the medical community, but to industry as well. At this point, the real news is not the fact that people want to make pot legal, but that the idea is still unthinkable to most Americans. For Mary Rathbun and others who are familiar with pot's many uses (besides smoking it for a recreational "high"), its official status as an outlaw plant seems patently absurd.

Marijuana is a Mexican term for the leaves and flowering buds of the hemp plant. Used for thousands of years in China and India for its medicinal properties, Cannabis Sativa (the clinical name for marijuana) and its extracts were used by American doctors until 1937.

Hemp fibers were used for centuries to make cloth, paper, and most of the world's rope. Oil was extracted from its seeds for fuel and lubricants. American Colonists, including George Washington and Thomas Jefferson, grew hemp on their farms; Jefferson composed the early drafts of the Declaration of Independence on Hemp paper.

In the 1920s and '30s, at the same time that heroin and morphine addiction was causing alarm among the American public, newspapers began spreading stories about the "killer weed" marijuana. Marijuana use was associated with blacks and Mexican immigrants and was often linked to the "savage" behavior associated with these groups.

Harry Anslinger, the commissioner of the Federal Bureau of Narcotics, took up the cause against marijuana and lobbied congress for its prohibition. Using what he called his "gore files", a collection of sensationalist news stories with such headlines as "Marijuana makes Fiends of Boys in 30 Days," he persuaded congress to pass anti-marijuana legislation in 1937, ignoring the protests of the hemp industry.

Over time, numerous studies have debunked the claims of Anslinger and other anti-hemp partisans that marijuana causes antisocial behavior or acts as a stepping stone to more harmful drugs. In 1988, an administrative judge of the Drug Enforcement Agency ruled that marijuana was proven to be medically valuable and extremely safe, not only safer than most prescription drugs but safer than many foods, including potatoes. This decision was upheld by the Federal Court of Appeals in April, 1991, but the DEA has refused to accept the recommendations of its own judge.

The fact that many people still believe Harry Anslinger's fictitious assertions demonstrates his skill as a propagandist. Of course, his cause has been aided more recently by the

Brownie Mary and San Francisco's finest

DEA and other well-intentioned but misguided antidrug crusaders who confuse marijuana with genuinely harmful substances like crack, amphetamines and heroin. Even though two former pot smokers now occupy the white house, the sheer magnitude of the Reagan/Bush "drug war" has made a pro-pot stance politically untouchable.

Consider the efforts of the Partnership for a Drug-Free America, which is conducting "the largest pro-bono media effort in the nation's history." Its anti-marijuana ads are playing on Television and the *New York Times* so frequently as to make one forget there's such a thing as crack. The Partnership's press kit looks like a subtle version of something out of Orwell's *1984*. Many of its print ads use the clearly McCarthyite tactic of warning that unemployment looms for anyone using illegal substances, not because of diminished job performance but because of drug-testing programs.

One ad meant for a younger audience labels a joint "dweeb weed", meaning that juvenile pot smokers will be ostracized by peers who are influenced by these same ads.

There's an ad that links pot use directly to cocaine use, while another places a small pile of marijuana between lines of coke and a hypodermic syringe. A full-page *New York Times* ad shows crack vials, a heroin needle, a bag of coke, a rolled joint, an unrolled joint, a bong and loose pot; alongside truly addictive and deadly substances, pot gets double or triple billing from the Partnership. There's even an ad linking casual pot users with dead police officers. The "reefer madness" contingent definitely got their substances confused on this one.

Finally, there's a page that compares pot to toxic pollutants spewing forth from factory chimneys. The tragic irony here is that pulp mills emit vast amounts of toxins as they turn forests into computer paper, while the technology exists to turn pot into paper more cheaply and easily without involving bleach or dioxin. Hemp paper is quite feasible — it is currently manufactured in China and is the cheapest acid-free paper available. Meanwhile, anti-marijuana laws prevent the United States from producing this valuable trade resource.

Ironically, advocates of legalization have often helped the cause of their opponents by portraying pot chiefly as a recreational drug. NORML (National Organization for the Reform of Marijuana Laws)

This is the weed that Jack bought. Jack got it from Bobby. Bobby is Jack's best friend. Bobby bought it from some dude down south who blew away two cops to get it over the border. Just for Jack. Tony knew this neighborhood connection—Sid or someone. Sid made a deal with a guy downtown who scored it from some dude down south. Tony bought it from his pal at school.

played into the hands of the DEA for more than a decade by defending the "right" to smoke pot as a civil liberties issue. The idea of pleasure as a constitutional right has never had much of a following in the United States; the historical example of alcohol prohibition should teach us that much. Even under prohibition, however, the thought of banning alcohol from hospitals and factories never crossed anyone's mind. To do so would have been pure folly, undermining whatever real support prohibition had behind it.

The real tragedy of the legalization movement is the way it has been portrayed (or ignored) by the press, and consequently misunderstood by the American people. Pot is treated as a joke rather than as a real issue. Instead of hearing about AIDS and cancer patients desperate for prescription pot, we hear about "smoke-ins" and raids on wealthy college students. Joke or not, billions of tax dollars are being spent enforcing laws that were passed under mistaken assumptions.

We forget that these same tax dollars put Mary Rathbun on trial and are plunging countless others into ruinous legal entanglements. Television viewers almost never hear about the near-warfare going on in the pot growing regions of the Pacific Northwest. In isolated rural communities, DEA commando units are trampling citizens' property rights as they bring the "drug war" home. For otherwise peaceful citizens who find themselves on the wrong end of the law, legalization is not a laughing matter.

By some estimates, efforts to eradicate marijuana and arrest its users constitute 50% of the DEA's enforcement budget. Should this really be a priority at a time when the nation can ill-afford to throw money away? A huge, untaxable, illegal trade in pot

continues even with prices skyrocketing, while the federal budget deficit grows more untamable. Meanwhile, whole forests are being consumed by the demand for wood and paper, yet hemp-based substitutes are within easy reach.

People with every known political viewpoint are asking why this country is in such bad shape. There is virtual unanimity of opinion that crime, the economy, and a failing health care system are undermining America's strength. With problems so widespread, the gospel of "no easy solutions" blinds everyone to the fact that there are simple steps that can be taken in the right direction. One such step is as plain as a hand held in front of our eyes, but we've been blindfolded for so long that we can't see it. It's so close, though . . . we can almost catch a whiff of it.

Wayne Jebian is researching for a book about the drug war. Contact him about pot busts and its consequences you've experienced at 655 Madison Ave., 7th Floor, New York, NY 10021. Confidentiality is guaranteed.

SKIRMISHES OF THE POT WAR

Wayne Jebian

Dennis Peron, author of Proposition P, San Francisco's medical pot law, has been arrested sixteen times on marijuana-related charges and was shot by a police officer during one of these busts. In the late 1970s, Peron authored Proposition W, a full marijuana legalization bill which was passed by the San Francisco electorate and was to be enforced by Mayor George Moscone and Supervisor Harvey Milk. Before Proposition W could be enacted, the two city officials were killed by an ex-police officer and political opponent Dan White, and the marijuana law fell by the wayside. At his trial, White pleaded temporary insanity brought on by eating too many twinkies and was given a lenient jail sentence. (Source: Dennis Peron).

Valerie Corrall of Santa Cruz, California, grew marijuana with the tacit approval of her doctor because it proved the most effective treatment for her epilepsy. In August, 1992, Valerie and her husband, Michael, were arrested and charged with felony marijuana cultivation. Instead of pleading guilty in exchange for leniency, she and her lawyer, Paul Meltzer, used medical necessity as a legal defense. Concurrent with the Corralls' trial, the County of Santa Cruz passed a medical marijuana bill modeled on San Francisco's Proposition P. Earlier this year, Valerie and Mike Corrall won their court case. As the first test case of a medical necessity defense, this precedent should put teeth into the Santa Cruz pot law as well as similar statutes elsewhere. (Source: Santa Cruz Good Times).

Bridget and Kevin Perry were arrested in September, 1988, for growing marijuana plants behind their home in Ossipee, New Hampshire. After pleading guilty to misdemeanors and paying a fine, they thought their ordeal was over. A month later, the Federal Government seized their home for "facilitating a drug crime," placing the Perrys among tens of thousands of individuals who have had their property seized through federal forfeiture laws. These laws allow law enforcement officials to confiscate property under any suspicion of wrongdoing, regardless of whether or not criminal charges have been filed. Since the assets seized are split between the federal government and local law enforcement agencies, this system has encouraged widespread abuse. For example, in Washington, D.C., police shake down black men and take whatever cash they are carrying, even when no drugs are found and no arrests are made. (Source: USA Today).

Donald Scott was killed on October 2, 1992 by a Los Angeles sheriff during a large scale raid on Scott's 200-acre ranch in Malibu, California. He was suspected of growing marijuana plants in treetop planters, even though overflights and illegal searches of his property yielded no hard evidence. The raid that resulted in Scott's death turned up no plants or drugs of any kind. Ventura County District Attorney Michael Bradbury concluded that the sheriffs used an illegal search warrant with the intent of seizing Scott's ranch by forfeiture, calling Donald Scott "an unfortunate victim of the war on drugs." Donald Scott's property did not become part of the $3 billion seized so far through civil forfeiture, but he lost something far more valuable, his life. (Source: *Village Voice*)

"Donny the Punk," a New York underground columnist, was arrested on December 27, 1976 in Jacksonville, North Carolina for felony possession of marijuana after an illegal search of his hotel room yielded 1/2 ounce of pot. Unable to raise $1500 cash bail, he spent the next several weeks in the Onslow County Jail. During his first night in the facility, Donny was gang-raped by eleven incarcerated Marines. Through the remainder of his stay, four Marines guarded Donny from the advances of the others in exchange for his services as a round-the-clock sex slave. At his hearing, the Judge decided to suppress the evidence (the 1/2 ounce of pot) because of the manner in which it was seized, and Donny was set free. (Source: Donny the Punk)

Brett Coleman Kimberlin, a federal prisoner originally from Indiana, claims to have sold marijuana to former Vice President Dan Quayle during the 1970s. After finding Kimberlin guilty of marijuana smuggling in 1979, authorities spuriously linked him to an unsolved series of bombings and murders in Indiana. During the last days of the 1988 presidential campaign, Kimberlin tried to hold a press conference concerning the Quayle story, but he was placed in "administrative detention," rendering him inaccessible to the outside world. The press conference was canceled by a direct order from the head of the Federal Bureau of Prisons after he had communicated with the Bush/Quayle campaign. Brett Kimberlin was subsequently denied parole despite his status as a model prisoner, and he remains behind bars to this day. (Source: *The New Yorker*)

OUR ERODING PRIVACY

Tony Lesce

Our right to privacy has been under attack by those we can call "control people," private individuals and government officials who strive to find rationalizations to support their intrusions into our lives. Some take advantage of "politically correct" trends, such as the "war on drugs," to institute greater invasions of our privacy, such as workplace urine testing. Others use economic rationalizations, such as cost to the health care system, to justify seat belt and motorcycle helmet laws.

Do We Have A Right to Our Own Bodies?

Controllers began with a simple premise: furthering public health is good for both individuals and the country. This led to mandatory eye drops for newborn babies, to guard against syphilitic infection and blindness, Some states passed laws mandating sterilization of the mentally retarded. Today's horizons are broader, with the advent of inexpensive tests for genetic defects that can be applied to adults and babies to screen for a variety of defects. Government-sponsored programs are not the real threat, because they're answerable to the people, at least in theory. Private organizations, such as employers, can be more aggressive in their screening programs. Motorola, for example, instituted random urine testing for even its long-time loyal employees. An increasing number of companies are using genetic screening to weed out those who might fall ill during their employment.

What employers don't tell applicants and employees is that urine samples also disclose other information, such as pregnancy and diabetes, as well as other medical conditions which may affect the hiring decision.

Genetic Testing

Genetic testing is a not science fiction, but fact, and while it holds promise for new medical advances, it presents unprecedented dangers to privacy. Some corporations already use genetic testing to weed out people with sensitivities to industrial chemicals, but the genetic information on individuals can also serve as a means of workplace discrimination, pre-screening for health insurance, etc. We're facing the prospect of a "genetic proletariat," denied well-paying employment, health and life insurance, and even credit, because of potential susceptibility to health problems originating in their genes.

Are We What We Eat?

Currently, medical consensus is that eating "right" can reduce the dangers from a variety of ailments. While there's no immediate prospect of a "cholesterol police," trends in private organizations provide a view of the future. Insurance carriers provide lower rates for non-smokers. It's only a minor step to include lower rates for those who eat a company-approved "healthy" diet, and to check up on clients by periodic blood tests. Of course, clients can refuse this invasion of their privacy, but insurance carriers can also refuse to insure them.

Intercepting Communications

The privacy of communications has long been held sacred. Interception of mail is illegal, and even postal inspectors cannot open first-class letters without a court order. Radio communications have always been fair game, however, especially in wartime. Enemy interception of radio communications became so common that one exasperated German general stated during WWII that "Anyone who uses the radio commits treason!" Civilians, on the other hand, can expect anything they say on any sort of wireless phone to be overheard by eavesdroppers.

Wiretap laws in this country have see-sawed, at times allowing official agencies to intercept communications, and alternately, restricting wiretaps to those legalized by warrants. However, technology has outstripped the laws, and for practical purposes, wiretap laws are obsolete. Several years ago, in Missouri, a neighbor overheard a drug dealer arranging a sale on his portable phone, which used the same frequency as the neighbor's. A court upheld this evidence, stating that radio-phones were not subject to the same expectations of privacy as land-lines.

This year, in Arizona, a radio ham intercepted a cellular phone conversation during which two teenagers discussed poisoning their

teacher. He tape-recorded the conversation and turned the tape over to police. This resulted in a prosecution for conspiracy to murder, and the privacy issue never surfaced.

Although both cases of communication interception described about ended up in court because the accused were planning illegal actions over the air, these cases point up that all our radio communications are vulnerable because many people routinely eavesdrop. Any legislation against casual eavesdropping would be impossible to enforce, and you might be discussing a very personal topic on your portable or cellular telephone, for the unintentional entertainment of anyone tuned in to your frequency.

It doesn't matter that you have nothing illegal to hide. You may not want neighbors to know the details of your wife's hysterectomy, or that your son had failed in school. If you're a businessman, anything you say on the air is available to eaves-droppers, which may include your competitors. It's not necessary to carry out industrial espionage by bugging a competitor's office, if he discusses sensitive information on a radio-telephone. You simply listen in and obtain your information at no risk of detection or prosecution for trespassing.

Discrimination in Employment.

In theory, employers are forbidden to ask applicants about their age, religion, political views, pregnancy, ethnic background, etc. In practice, fair employment laws are almost impossible to enforce. Skilled interviewers have devised methods of asking oblique questions to ferret out such privileged information. The interviewer doesn't ask the applicant's religion or status of young children. Instead, he asks whether the person can work evenings or weekends, or whether there are any reasons he or she may not make overnight business trips.

Surveillance And Lists

Your name may be on a police list, if your car was parked near a political or homosexual rally, as happened to a Phoenix man several years ago. To his surprise, he was listed in the police computer as a high AIDS risk because officers had copied license plate numbers of all vehicles parked near where a homosexual group was holding a picnic.

Police agencies have for years routinely copied license numbers of vehicles parked near political rallies and meetings of suspected organized crime figures. Lending your vehicle to someone who uses it to attend one of these meetings could easily result in your name being added to a computerized list maintained by a police agency.

A tiny minority of computer bulletin boards have been used for illegal purposes, such as pirating copyrighted software and child pornography. This has led to wide-spread police surveillance of bulletin boards, with undercover agents logging on merely to see what the service offers. However, very few prosecutions have resulted from this extensive surveillance.

It gets worse when police leak information to a private group. A San Francisco detective provided information to the Jewish Anti-Defamation League, which conducts nationwide surveillance of political groups and individuals it considers inimical to its cause. Some of this information may have gone to Israeli security authorities, as one American of Arab descent found himself detained in Tel Aviv while on a trip to visit relatives on the West Bank.

What's especially dangerous is that some of the information in police intelligence files is inaccurate. Leaking such information to private groups or agents of foreign governments can result in reprisals for people who are erroneously listed as members of a political group.

The Future is Bleak

Modern technology offers both public and private groups more ways to intrude into areas that used to be sacrosanct. More "privacy" laws won't help, because technology always runs ahead of the law, and loopholes are easy to find. Our private lives will continue to be open to both public and corporate snoops.

---

*Tony Lesche is author of **The Privacy Poachers**, reviewed in **Gauntlet** #4 (Loompanics Unlimited, 1992)*

The Most Personal Public Secret of All

Jil McIntosh

Early in 1958, a young woman working for an insurance company in a large New England state had an affair with a co-worker. She became pregnant. She told him and insisted that he marry her, but he had a secret of his own: he was already married, and his own wife had a child on the way.

The news devastated her and she almost had a nervous breakdown. She could not tell her old-country Hungarian parents about the pregnancy, so she used the breakdown as an excuse to go with a girlfriend to Florida, supposedly to recuperate. In Daytona Beach, she reluctantly went to a social worker and made arrangements to give the baby up for adoption. In February of 1959, the child was born and taken from her, and eleven days later it left the hospital to begin life with a new set of parents.

As you may have gathered, that baby girl was me. And unless the state of Florida drastically changes its laws, or I spend an enormous amount of time and money with no guarantee of success, that is all I well ever know.

The powers that be have decided that someone *might* be upset if I knew the truth, and have ruled that my parents' right to privacy is more important than my right to know. But people should know that ultimately,

they are responsible for the consequences of their own actions. I am sure that my mother did not intend to become pregnant, and that giving me up was both selfless and the hardest thing she had ever done. Nevertheless, the consequences of the parents' actions was a living, breathing, thinking human being with a need to know her identity, and I should not have to live my life in ignorance because some people believe that their responsibility to that consequence ended when a piece of paper was signed and I went home with someone else.

How strong is the need to know? Many people brush it off, and some equate my need with a total disregard for everything my adoptive family has done for me. Garbage. I love my adoptive family as much as anyone could, and my crusade to discover who I am is no more of an insult to them than someone researching her great-grandparents is belittling her mother and dad. My birth parents and their families are linked marginally to all of my family and yet are mine alone, in the same way that my brother's wife's family is linked to him. Being completely accepted as a family member by another group totally unrelated to his own does absolutely nothing to sever his ties with his own parents and siblings, just as my need to touch with my birth parents would never affect my love for the family who made me their own thirty-five years ago.

Is there really a "need" to know? Yes, even among those who were not adopted, as evidenced by the booming business of genealogy and family crests. Multicultural programs exist to educate people in the customs of their ancestors, and immigrants ensure that the languages and foods of their homelands are passed along to their children. For the adopted, there are hundreds of organizations dedicated to bringing original families together, and many lawyers and private investigators have made this type of work their specialty. Open the newspapers of any major city and count how many classified advertisements are pleas for information on long-lost relatives.

It doesn't stop with ancestry; the need to continue the bloodline — the "real" bloodline — is just as strong. People are often so desperate for their "own" children that they will try any type of reproductive technology offered, regardless of its cost, discomfort or difficulty. Rather than adopt, they will hire a surrogate to carry a child that will be genetically theirs. Even people who have successfully adopted children usually keep trying to produce one of their own. Couples who have to "resort" to adoption generally want an infant that looks like them, and many perpetrate that myth even further by lying to the child about its birth (as happened with me). There is no doubt that humans need to be able to find their proper place in a long, unbroken line

> The humiliation associated with the search can be just as bad as not knowing anything.

of descent, a right that adopted children are so often denied simply because authorities don't understand, or downplay, that requirement.

The humiliation associated with the search can be just as bad as not knowing anything. My birth records are sealed, but no one will define that term for me, and I don't know if it means the envelope is glued shut or if only certain people are allowed to look at it. I know beyond a shadow of a doubt that it means *I* can't. That is the cruel part of all of this: somewhere in a Florida courthouse is a document that contains everything about *my* mother and father, the circumstances of *my* birth, the circumstances of *my* adoption, about *me*, and I am not allowed to see it.

When I started questioning the courthouse about my adoption, I was told about the existence of the document and given some non-identifying information from it. When I wrote back to them regarding it, I was informed by the circuit judge that "they cannot locate it". A nice way to say that someone lost it, and my letters asking if it has been found have never been answered.

Since I knew the hospital I had been born in, I wrote to their records department and asked them about the baby girls born that day. Their reply stated that "due to the sensitive nature of this record, I'm unable to release any information regarding it". Their records are not sealed, and undoubtedly their clerk looked through it to determine its nature. She probably read all of the information I have searched for these last eight years and now she knows my name, my parents, all about me. Any-

It is the height of irresponsibility for anyone to give or accept sperm or ovum under the cloak of secrecy.

has decided that a sealed document about me must remain a secret.

Adoption records must be unsealed and made available, and it should be done immediately while there is still time for those searching. Birth parents who give up their children, no matter how difficult and selfless their act, must realize that they are not giving away a puppy, but a human being who will have questions. One of the consequences of adoption must be the possibility that at some time in the future, that human being will come to its birth parents demanding that those questions be answered.

If necessary, combine the laws regarding open records with laws prohibiting adoptees or birth parents from demanding inheritance as their birthright; that should help to allay the fears of people who fight against open records only because they see a monetary value attached to everything.

The right to know must also extend to all situations where children are denied knowledge of their natural parents, including reproductive technologies such as artificial insemination or egg donation using anonymous donors.

It is the height of irresponsibility for anyone to give or accept sperm or ovum under the cloak of secrecy. While my search has been long and difficult and not yet fruitful, the information is there. The child of an anonymous donor cannot even hope for that and is completely unable to fulfill the need and the right to know his or her identity.

Knowing firsthand the questions and uncertainties created by adoption, and viewing as a "last resort only" the rejection of a child from its family line when it is given up, I am unable to justify the intentional creation of a child outside of its biological family. In my perfect

one who argues for sealed adoption records should know how it feels when a total stranger knows more about you than you do.

There are as many reasons for wanting to know as there are people searching, and the fact that some adoptees and birth parents might use the information for harassment is not sufficient grounds to deny everyone involved their right to know. My main reason, although I find if difficult to explain why it's important to me, is that I want to know what my name was. (One document I was allowed to see was entitled "Adoption of female infant Keilback", but no one at the courthouse would tell me if this was the name of my father, my mother, or the social worker, and a search of hundreds of telephone books has not turned up this unusual name.) I desperately want to write to my mother and just let her know that everything turned out well, although oddly enough I don't crave a face-to-face meeting. I would like to see her photograph. And I would like to know about my siblings; since my father's wife was pregnant I probably have at least one. A name and a couple of family members: something millions of people take for granted, and something denied to me and others like me because a judge world, couples would have to live with their infertility; no matter how painful their situation, it would not give them the right to produce a child who would have to live with the consequences all of its life.

Of course, realistically I know that the "me-first" attitude will always prevail, and donor insemination will always remain an option to people who believe that their right to procreate by whatever means possible outweighs the rights of our society. That being the case, information on sperm and egg donors must be taken, and made available freely whenever the child wishes to know.

Undoubtedly the fear of this knowledge would prevent a few people from donating, and many would argue that men and women would live in dread of the day that a child created from their donations might knock on their door and announce themselves. I hope this happens. People who donate eggs and sperm for whatever reason have to realize that those products will be used to create another human being (or series of human beings) who might one day have questions about themselves. It is criminal for people to think that they can blithely give away their genetic makeup without having to answer to the consequences, and that people could then use these donations to create life without telling those children about their origins.

Since a single sperm donation has the capacity to produce many children, all with the same father, a mandatory donor registry would also lessen the risk of a very real possibility: that of half-siblings unknowingly marrying and producing children of their own. Such a possibility reinforces the need not only for donor identification but also for parents who fully understand the importance of revealing the "secret" to the child.

No one has the right to keep secrets when they concern the very person they are being kept from. I am sure my birth mother did the best thing for me, and I am grateful for it. However, her selfless act does not mean that the state has the right to grant her immunity from my questions, as it now does. She knew the consequences of her act; I had no say whatsoever, and still don't. I am still the person who must know that strangers know more about me than I do; I am still the person who must hire a lawyer, and investigator or an agency to uncover information that others take for granted. I am still the person who looks in the mirror and cannot fully understand what she sees.

If any of the members of my natural family recognize me through this article, I urge you to write me in care of this magazine. Ironically enough, like so many people who share my situation, I may find the answers to the most personal secret I carry only by parading it in the most public of places. I can live with that, though. Once you've been told that you can't read your own documents, that others have access to records you can't see, and that your files have been lost by a clerk you'll never meet, believe me: the rest is easy.

Jil McIntosh is a Canadian freelance writer.

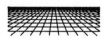

DOWN FOR THE COUNT

Mark Shaw

In his short, but explosive career as a boxer, ex-heavyweight champion Mike Tyson never met an opponent as tough as the criminal justice system.

Tyson's accuser, Desiree Washington, learned that even when a jury says you won, in the end, somehow that win is tainted so badly that the world still wonders whether you were lying.

Even his shocking K.O. by flash-in-the-pan boxer James "Buster" Douglas in Tokyo must seem mild in comparison with the knockout punch delivered by the Indiana judicial system. To his incredible dismay, that system hit Tyson with a pro-prosecution judge, prosecutors who withheld critical evidence, a borderline-incompetent defense trial attorney, a jury that seemed more swayed by Tyson's bad boy public image than the incomplete facts in the case, and loud-mouthed appellate counsel who publicly ridiculed the Indiana courts and judges.

To be sure, Mike Tyson's advisers are responsible for many of the decisions that led him directly to prison, but the former heavyweight boxing champion of the world still must sit in his prison cell today, and wonder what the hell happened to him. From the moment fate brought the ex-champ in contact with beauty contestant Desiree Washington, to February 15th when his appeal was heard in Indianapolis, Tyson has taken more shots to the jaw than a has-been fighter.

Tyson's fall from grace began when he somehow convinced the eighteen-year old Washington to accompany him to a hotel room in downtown Indianapolis at two o'clock in the morning on July 19, 1992. After some harmless chit-chat, Washington and Tyson then had sex either consensually or forcibly, depending on which version of the story one believes.

The circumstances surrounding that sex act thus set up the only critical legal issue to be decided — whether Mike Tyson was guilty of the illegal crime of rape.

Tyson truly believed he was innocent. Learning from past mistakes involving his celebrity status and altercations with "groupies," he made his sexual intentions perfectly clear several times to Washington by in effect telling her: I want to fuck you. When she nevertheless accepted his invitation to leave her hotel room in the middle of the night, and then kissed him in the limousine when they met, Tyson knew he and Washington were on the same wavelength.

When Desiree Washington voluntarily came in and sat on the bed in his hotel room, Tyson was even more sure of himself. After the beauty queen went to the bathroom (where she removed a panty shield), and then returned to the bed, he was positive that her intentions were to have sex with him.

Desiree Washington truly believed she was raped. In spite of Tyson's blatant sexual innuendoes both to her and other beauty contestants during preliminary competition for the 1992 Miss Black America Pageant, Washington had only joined Tyson to see the sights of the city. When Tyson said that he had to pick up something at the hotel, Washington went up to Tyson's hotel room, intending to stay briefly and leave.

Washington also knew she made her intentions clear by telling Tyson she "wasn't that kind of girl" when he tried to kiss her while they sat on the bed. She had merely removed the panty shield because "her time was coming," and was shocked to see Tyson sitting on the bed wearing only flimsy briefs when she came out of the bathroom.

When Tyson grabbed her, and pulled her down, Washington told him "no," that "I have a future," and "I don't want a baby." Nevertheless, Tyson forced himself on her, and raped her in spite of her cries for him to stop.

Putting aside all of the peripheral issues, and based simply on the differing facts in the two stories, this was a classic case of "he-says, she-says," with the outcome of the case hinging upon who a jury would believe.

To combat the charges, Tyson was advised by his loquacious promoter Don King, himself once a convicted felon, that he needed the best lawyer money could buy. This would be the first piece of disastrous advice that the ex-champ would receive, and the selection of famed trial lawyer Vincent Fuller would trigger a spiraling descent that would ultimately send Tyson *Down For The Count*.

More than any other event, the decision to select Fuller, a brilliant Federal Court white-collar crime attorney, but a soon-to be-out-of-his-league barrister in the down and dirty county criminal courts of Indianapolis, would be a most regrettable one for Tyson. Even King would later admit that Fuller's performance was most disappointing, which was a gross understatement when compared with the critical assessment by noted legal experts, and in private by trial Judge Patricia Gifford.

And what of the judge? With six criminal courts in Marion County, Tyson could have landed before any one of six judges, but both fate and an intentional decision by Marion County Prosecutor Jeffrey Modisett made certain that Judge Gifford would rule over Tyson's case.

In addition to the poor performance from defense counsel Fuller at trial, Tyson would be tried in a court run by not only a conservative law and order judge, but one that was a former prosecutor who had specialized in of all things: rape cases. In fact, Gifford had co-written the Indiana Rape Shield Law that prohibits defense attorneys from delving into the past life of rape victims. (Gifford would later agree with a rape-shield argument from the prosecution prohibiting them from introducing evidence regarding Washington's sexual history.)

And just how had Gifford ended up with Tyson's case? Besides relying on a questionable pro-prosecution Indiana procedure which allowed criminal cases to be rotated among the six courts, Modisett guaranteed that Gifford would be Tyson's trial judge when he sent the Washington case to a special grand jury instead of allowing it to go through the usual grand jury procedure.

When Fuller's asinine attempt to ward off a grand jury indictment by allowing Tyson to testify failed miserably, Tyson was now in the hands of Gifford, who would rule on all pretrial and trial motions, preside over the trial itself, and of course be the judge who would sentence Tyson if he were found guilty of the charges against him.

While the defense did unsuccessfully question the procedure as to how the judge was selected, Tyson's attorneys surprisingly did not request a change of judge. Predictably, when all of the motions for discovery, and other procedural issues were heard prior to the trial, Judge Gifford awarded the defense the small victories while awarding the prosecution the big ones.

To combat the anticipated brilliance of Fuller, prosecutor Modisett brought in a big gun himself to try the case. Undefeated at trial since the early seventies, fiery special prosecutor Greg Garrison and his cowboy boots joined legal tactician Barb Trathen to set up the formidable team that would face-off with Fuller.

Meanwhile, Desiree Washington was preparing for future legal battles herself by signing an attorney retainer fee agreement with Rhode Island lawyer Ed Gerstein, who explained to her the ramifications of filing a civil suit for monetary damages against Tyson after the criminal case was over.

Whether prosecutors ever actually saw the retainer agreement remains unclear. However, there is no question that they knew of its existence, since questions about the agreement were asked of Washington in the presence of Garrison and Trathen at a mock cross-examination of Washington held prior to trial.

What the prosecutors, or Washington's own money-hungry private attorney told her to say about the agreement or her intentions to sue Tyson is unknown, but Washington seemed confused and unsure when she was questioned in pre-trial depositions, and at trial.

Whatever the case, Modisett's office may therefore have committed prosecutorial misconduct by either deliberately concealing the existence of the agreement from the defense, or by promoting false testimony in advising Washington to be vague regarding questions about the fee agreement.

The defense thus never requested the document in its discovery motions, and were not able to present it to the jury at trial. Unfortunately for Tyson, the confused Fuller never really asked the right questions during cross-examination of Washington, or her parents, at trial, but the evasive answers given were still either misleading, or downright perjurious, depending on one's viewpoint.

At trial, Fuller continued with his pattern of handling Tyson's defense like a first year law student. Due to his regrettable decision to fire the jury selection experts who had successfully assisted defense lawyer Roy Black in the William Kennedy Smith case, Fuller and his cohorts were left to haphazardly select the jury that would decide Tyson's fate.

To the amazement of legal experts covering the trial, Fuller allowed an ex-Marine, whose *voir dire* answers were very pro-prosecution, to sit on the jury. This shocking error was a reminder of famed attorney F. Lee Bailey's fatal mistake in the Patty Hearst case when he allowed an Air force colonel to sit in judgment of Hearst. No one, of course, was surprised when the ex-Marine, who was later selected as the jury foreman, led the deliberation efforts to convict Tyson.

Fuller's overall trial strategy was even more questionable. Although he'd never tried a sex crimes case in his career, Fuller believed that if he could convince the jurors that a) Tyson was a bad boy/sexual animal; b)Tyson clearly showed Washington he only had sex on his mind; and c) because Tyson was so bad and told Washington he wanted sex, then Washington knew what she was in for, and must have consented to the sex.

Instead of concentrating on the obvious question in everyone's mind — what was Washington doing in Tyson's hotel room at 2:00 a.m. taking off her panty shield if she didn't want to have sex, Fuller decided to fight his client's war by presenting the "Tyson, the sexual animal," argument in combination with his allegation that Washington was a money hungry, scorned lover who filed rape charges simply because she was after Tyson's fame and fortune.

While his argument regarding Washington's money motives could have been stronger if he had possessed the retainer fee agreement, Fuller was continually outclassed and outfoxed by Garrison and Trathen at trial. With the comfort of knowing Gifford would handle any major legal skirmishes in their favor, the two prosecutors concentrated on establishing a friendly rapport with the mostly all-white, hometown jurors. The veteran prosecutors then went on to portray Tyson as a rich celebrity who would have done anything to get his way with the naive, unsuspecting Washington.

Even though Fuller botched most of the pre-trial and trial matters, and ineffectively cross-examined Washington, many jurors said later they still had reasonable doubt in their minds as to whether Tyson was guilty after the close of the State's case. Therefore, if the defense had simply rested, Tyson might now once again be the filthy-rich heavyweight champion of the world, instead of a sixty-five-cent-per-day broom handler at the Indiana Youth Center.

Despite Tyson's bumbling, and at times, downright pitiful performance as a witness at the Grand Jury, Fuller decided Mike needed to tell his story to the jurors once and for all. This ill-conceived decision, like so many others by Fuller, turned sour when Tyson was picked apart by the cagey Garrison, and made to appear the lying fool in front of the twelve people who would ultimately judge him.

With the ex-Marine at the helm, the jury of eight men and four women (just two were black), took less than ten hours to deliberate, before finding Michael Tyson guilty of one count of rape and two counts of criminal deviate conduct.

Post-trial reports from jurors raised speculation that one smart-aleck juror played "devils advocate", and misled others with his intentions causing two of the women jurors to change their vote to guilty. In addition, one juror, Michael Wettig, admitted that when the jury could not decide Tyson's guilt or innocence as to the deviate conduct charges, they simply "guessed", contrary to law, that "if Tyson was guilty of rape, he must be guilty of the other charges too."

From the point in the trial where Tyson had testified, there was no question that the former champ was a goner. To be sure, fate had brought together a complicated set of circumstances that served to slam the cell door behind Tyson. In the final analysis, though, he had been caught in a trap set for him by cunning players in an unbalanced criminal justice system that produced the only result possible — a rape conviction and prison term for the unknowing twenty-five year old.

Seconds after Tyson was convicted, another famed attorney, appellate counsel Alan Dershowitz, leaped into the fray. Not only a master of the legal technicalities so critical to gaining reversal for an

RORSCHACH TEST: What do you see?

imprisoned client, but a public relations expert as well, the Harvard professor immediately chastised the entire Indiana criminal justice system, including all of the judges, trial and appellate, for their lack of knowledge of correct judicial procedures.

Hopping from Maury Povich to Larry King to Morton Downey, Tyson's new advocate launched an outlandish public relations crusade designed to paint Tyson as the downtrodden victim of a prejudicial judge, prejudicial prosecutor, and a prejudicial jury that would have never voted to convict the ex-champ if they had been presented with all of the facts.

Forgetting all sense of legal or moral ethics, Dershowitz labeled Washington as a "liar, a perjurer, and a whore" who only accused Tyson of rape in order to benefit financially from a civil suit, and/or money from the sale of the movie and book rights.

Having successfully lessened the boxer's chances for a fair shake in the appellate court by bad-mouthing Indiana's court system and its judges, and through his vicious personal attacks on Washington's character, Dershowitz finally argued Tyson's appeal before three appellate justices in mid-February.

In front of Justices Sue Shields, Jonathan Robertson, and Patrick Sullivan, the relentless Dershowitz argued that Tyson should have his rape conviction reversed, and be awarded a new trial based on the following arguments:

1. Trial Judge Patricia J. Gifford erred by blocking testimony from witnesses who might have challenged

the credibility of accuser Desiree Washington.

2. Gifford's refusal to allow the jury to hear an instruction regarding "mistake of fact," or "reasonable belief" concerning whether Tyson believed Washington wanted to have sex with him.

3. Gifford should have prevented jurors from listening to Washington's call to 911 reporting the alleged attack. The defense claims Washington invented the attack to sue Tyson, and that the call might have been part of the scheme.

4. The prosecution committed misconduct by concealing from the defense an attorney-fee agreement for book and film rights to Washington's story.

5. Prosecutors manipulated court selection procedure to pick a supposedly sympathetic judge.

Of these arguments, the three conservative law and order judges seemed most intrigued by the refusal of Judge Gifford to offer the "state of mind" instruction to the jury.

To support his contention that the jury needed to be guided by this important instruction, Dershowitz legitimately pointed out that the evidence at trial (specifically the testimony of a hospital chaplain that there was "some sort of participation" between Tyson and Washington) strongly indicated that Tyson reasonably believed that Washington wanted to have sex with him, despite her protestations to the contrary.

The State argued that, in fact, Washington said "no" to Tyson several times thus negating the potential effect of any instruction. The justices were left then to consider whether, under the guidelines of the absent instruction, the jury could have acquitted Tyson if he mistakenly believed Washington wanted sex.

While Dershowitz seemed on point with regard to the jury instruction argument, the outspoken appellate counsel may very well have damaged the effect of two other important arguments for Tyson. These involved his misstatements concerning the facts regarding the exclusion of the witnesses argument, and the alleged perjury by Washington involving the attorney fee agreement.

In spite of knowledge to the contrary, Dershowitz continued to wave the banner about the potential of the three witnesses who supposedly saw Washington and Tyson "necking" prior to their entering The Canterbury Hotel. Dershowitz's contention was adverse to the trial record, which indicated that there was only one witness who allegedly saw the "necking" between the couple, and there are even disputes as to whether that witness was even at the hotel on the night of the rape.

As for the attorney retainer fee agreement, Dershowitz alleged that Washington had her sights set on "movie and book rights" when, in fact, the retainer agreement itself clearly shows that it was nothing more than an agreement to retain general legal services of lawyer Gerstein.

Playing fast and foolish, Dershowitz not only soiled further his own reputation that once was impeccable, but lessened the chances for the remainder of his arguments to be taken seriously by the justices. Such conduct indicates that Dershowitz did not learn well from the mistakes of his predecessor Fuller, who also attempted to be a know-it-all, big shot from the East coast, whose overconfidence and aloofness never played well in Indiana.

Through it all, Mike Tyson, convict #922335, remains in prison where he mops the floor and passes out equipment in the weight room to his fellow inmates. Don King, Whitney Houston, Arsenio Hall, and Spike Lee come by to console him while Dershowitz, like Fuller before him, drains the former champ's bank account.

Reversing the conviction is, of course, a long shot, and only the justices know whether Tyson will see the light of day before the Summer of 1995. Regardless of the outcome of the appeal, Tyson's case will be remembered as one that brought many difficult an important social issues to a public that is often reluctant to even admit that these issues exist.

To begin with, was a rich celebrity singled out by overzealous prosecutors because of his fame and fortune, and was he wrongfully accused by a woman who simply sought fame and fortune herself?

Did a young black woman go from being the accuser to the accused, as her name was dragged through the mud by those who felt she falsely accused the celebrity of rape?

While Tyson must by responsible for his own actions, his advisers and legal counsel made decisions for him that, more than anything else, placed the ex-champ behind bars.

Whether his conviction is reversed or not, Tyson has had to pay the piper for his unfortunate acts. In truth, however, he has been represented by a trial defense counsel who should have never taken the case, and an appellate counsel who has gone way beyond the boundaries of accepted judicial ethics.

Further, Tyson's case was heard by a well-intentioned judge who either should have removed herself from presiding over the defense based on sound arguments regarding her pro-prosecution/rape case background.

Tyson, of course, was also up against win-at-all-costs prosecutors who apparently played keep-away with a critical piece of evidence, and a jury who was stacked against him, and may have arrived at his guilty verdict contrary to law.

On the other hand, Washington may very well have fallen prey to a private attorney who had Tyson dollar signs dancing in his head, and to headline-seeking prosecutors who led her down a path of half-truths concerning the attorney fee agreement.

In the end, Tyson, and Washington as well, have suffered from their fateful encounter. He has lost his freedom and, most likely, his career, and she, her dignity and sense of privacy.

While no one, except for the two combatants, knows what really happened between them, both put their trust in a legal system that promises truth and justice for all. Unfortunately, most of the critical participants in that very system used both Tyson and Washington as mere pawns, and concentrated on either filling their pockets with gold, or enhancing their own careers.

Mike Tyson and Desiree Washington both sought simple justice, but instead became victims themselves, caught in a criminal justice system that denied them the very justice they sought.

Down for the Count: The Shocking Truth Behind the Mike Tyson Rape Trial, published in 1993 is available through Sagamore Publishing (phone: 800-327-5557)

No Sympathy for Tyson

Richard G. Carter

In the early '60s that were my mid-20s, Charles (Sonny) Liston — a burly ex-con known as the "big ugly bear," was, arguably, the baddest cat in America. He was big and he was mean and he was black.

A renowned cop-beater from St. Louis with 18 arrests on his record, Liston stepped out of jail and into pro boxing to get paid for bashing heads. But even as he knocked out people left and right and never, ever cracked a smile, rumors of his mob ties persisted.

This terrifying fellow was a dynamite puncher and, along the way, invented the steely-eyed stare in pre-fight ring-center that has become commonplace. His first round KO — in 1962 — of the revered Floyd Patterson, won him the heavyweight championship of the world. When he served up a virtual replay a year later, Sonny's status was solidified as the man you'd want least to encounter in a dark alley.

The Liston fists faded from the scene in 1965 after the second of two tainted losses (especially the second) to his nemesis, Muhammad Ali. Following a winning comeback, he died in Las Vegas in 1971 at age 39. The official verdict was natural causes, although his body contained traces of narcotics. Some feel he fell victim to the mob.

Now comes Mike Tyson who, at age 26, seems hell-bent on making fearsome old Sonny look like a choirboy. And yet, as irresponsible as his outside-the-ring behavior has been, Iron Mike — who acts like he's got cement between his ears — has been regularly defended by some in the news media that I respect, and should know better.

It would be impossible to cite all of this immature young man's public indiscretions — stunts he pulled *prior* to his conviction for raping 18-year-old Desiree Washington in 1992, which got him six years in the slam in Indiana. But a partial roll call includes:

- Sucker-punching boxer Mitch (Blood) Green at 5 a.m. on a Harlem street in a fit of pique.
- Pinching the behinds of young ladies at a New York City disco.
- Making obscene gestures at a female court reporter during a court appearance concerning his managerial contract.
- Ramming his car into a tree near his Catskill (N.Y.) home in what some called a love-sick suicide attempt.
- Bragging about banging around his then wife, actress Robin Givens, in their home in New Jersey.
- Getting into a traffic accident in his expensive car on a New York street and then *giving* the car to cop who happened by.

And on and on and on.

Yes, yes, I know all about Tyson's deprived childhood — how he grew up in tough-as-nails Brownsville (in Brooklyn) and succumbed to the wicked ways of its oh-so mean streets. Of course, current heavyweight king Riddick Bowe grew up there at the same time and, as of now, is guilty of nothing besides fighting mostly stiffs and an ill-advised, tiresome imitation of the legendary Ali.

I believe the problem with Iron Mike is that *he* believes he really *is* "the baddest man on the planet." Which, in his mind, gives him the prerogative — no, the "right" — to kick ass and take names.

Too bad we no longer have universal military service — you know, the draft. A couple or three years in the Army, where he might have gotten some of that piss and vinegar knocked out of him, would have done Tyson a lot of good. The same goes for Bill Clinton — that's another story.

And as a proud African-American, I take particular umbrage at Tyson's boorish behavior — and that anyone would consider him a positive role model. Of course, this is a factor some of his white, well-intentioned apologists in the news media can't relate to.

My bottom line is this: When it came to out-and-out meanness, the storied Sonny Liston — whom I interviewed in a children's hospital, of all places — will always be number one in the fight game. He was truly scary and, in my view, would have pounded Tyson into submission in the squared circle.

And Iron Mike? Just a bum. Nothing more. An immature bum who should confine his temper tantrums to inside the ring where, in all honesty, he had no peer in his time.

Outside the ring, Tyson's conduct over the years speaks for itself. In my opinion, based on the evidence, he deserved to be found guilty of rape and deserved the jail sentence he received.

Finally, in thinking about Tyson, I am reminded of a scene from *The Dirty Dozen* (1967) — a blowtorch of a movie. Near the beginning, Lee Marvin, as a rebellious Army major, and his commanding general (Ernest Borgine), are discussing the hanging of soldiers convicted of capital crimes:

"That's no way for anybody to go," says Marvin.

"Oh, the hell you say, Major," laughs Borgine. "Why, I know a lot of people should go *just* that way!"

You see, Father Flanagan had it wrong. That *is* such a thing as a bad boy. And Mike Tyson is a prime example.

At press time, a motion for a new trial had been filed on behalf of Tyson by the famed celebrity attorney and Harvard law professor, Alan Dershowitz. He argued to an Indiana appeals court that the trial judge, Patricia Gifford, erred by failing to tell the jury it shouldn't find Tyson guilty if he misconstrued Ms. Washington's "no" to mean "yes."

Dershowitz also contends that evidence exists that the young woman falsely accused one of her high school classmates of raping her in October 1989, and that police never got involved.

But all of this is neither here nor there as far as Mike Tyson, the bad boy, man-child goes.

Perhaps Tyson will get a new trial and be found not guilty for whatever reason. Perhaps it will be proven that Ms. Washington is a scheming gold-digger. This will not change the simple fact that outside the ring, Iron Mike is a menace. Case closed.

---

*Richard G. Carter, a former columnist with the **New York Daily News** is a freelance writer.*

Sticks & Stones Do Break My Bones . . . Words Do Not Offend Me:

An Opposition to Hate Crime Legislation

Barbara Beebe

When I moved from San Francisco to the military town Fayetteville, NC, I was a bald-headed, butch, leather jacket-bearing dyke. The fact that social conformity was the least of my concerns turned out to be quite threatening to many local white males. After 8 months back in this town, I found myself the victim in what would be the first of two queer-bashings. In one instance I was attacked at a predominantly white bar where I was a regular customer. In this, as well as the second instance, people stood and watched without attempting to help me. In both instances, I phoned the police. In both situations, they refused to come to the scene of the crime.

No one considered these incidents to be the assaults they were. A white male who beats a black, queer-looking woman (who has the gall to socialize in traditionally white settings) may be verbally admonished for 'getting a little out of hand,' but no one wants to charge him with a crime. For years, and even now, this has been the typical response to many crimes committed against niggers, queers, cripples, old people and any-one else who finds themselves out-numbered, out-powered and/or despised in a social situation.

So what have organized groups of gays, women, blacks, liberals proposed as a way to alleviate this glaring disparity in justice and inequality of law enforcement? Hate crime legislation! I relate this story to show that hate crime legislation's most glaring downfall is that it does nothing to establish equality under the law for oppressed people.

A hate crime is an act committed against a person due to the social group in which the victim belongs. At least this is how proponents like to explain it. There are hate crime acts —as yet unspecified, vague and varied —and a rash of hate crime legislation. Everything from cross burning to verbal bigotry has been fingered as a hate crime. Despite the fact that the term is an oxymoron, like pornography it is a concept to be applied and not really a concrete thing.

The push for hate crime legislation is the logical and tragic extension of the hate speech movement. Hate speech legislation received a lethal blow when the Supreme Court struck down a St. Paul, Minnesota ordinance that banned cross-burnings and other expressions of racial bias. The court said this ordinance violated free speech because it sought to ban some viewpoints.

> The buzzword for the '90s is 'sensitivity,' folks. No one wants to be offended. No time. No way.

Proponents of hate crime legislation are overly concerned with the hatred and prejudice in the souls of folk, yet can only think to diminish or eradicate it by institutional punishment. Different opinions and beliefs expressed in a manner deemed inappropriate by the 'authorities' are supposedly deserving of harsher punishment than the commission of the real crime itself. If some people can't achieve cultural awareness and acceptance, we'll make the courts punish them.

Proponents of this legislation would have you believe that they honestly care about the lives and destinies of the oppressed. Their real reasons are less appealing. The buzzword for the '90s is 'sensitivity,' folks. No one wants to be offended. No time. No way. What used to be an issue of exposure, ridicule and desertion (remember "One in a Million" by Guns 'n' Roses?) has now become a crime (a group of cops want to sue Ice-T for "Cop Killer," claiming the song is a hate crime against officers!) It is a typical, liberal cover-up. It does nothing to change the social and eco-

nomic status of the oppressed and does everything to placate the masses. All the energy that has gone into collecting data on the number of "hate crimes" committed is wasted by attempting to create legislation in this over-litigated society.

There is a logical and rational case against hate crime legislation that has nothing to do with right v. left or conservative v. radical, but has a lot to do with the pain of freedom and the slow process of social compatibility and respect.

Proponents of hate crime legislation assume than one can actually attest and lay claim to hatred or bias by words expressed during the commission of a crime. The fact of the matter is, all crimes are motivated (whether expressed or not) by a form of bias, prejudice or hatred. Dr. Patricia J. Williams is correct when she states that "the attempt to split bias from violence has been society's most enduring and fatal rationalization."

What else could motivate crime? What is greed, but the bias toward those that have what you want? There is the well-known modus operandi of robbing the old. They are perceived (as a group) as being physically weak and not well-sighted. If some young punk robs an old lady, in the process calling her an old decrepit hag, is he guilty of a hate crime? Is there something wrong with simply charging him with robbery and calling him the creep that he is? Rapists typically rape women they perceive as weak. Are rapists now guilty of hate crime? We're already aware of the possible lurid profanities expressed during a rape. Does what rapists say matter as much as what they've done? With the myriad of problems that already complicate the judicial process, why initiate another element to what is already a crime?

Hate crime legislation attempts to punish the motivations and not the crime. The St. Paul, Minnesota case in point: a white kid burns a cross in the yard of the only black people in a neighborhood. What is he charged with? Not trespassing, vandalism or destruction of property. The poor fool is charged with a hate crime! Fortunately the Supreme Court ruled the ordinance unconstitutional. However, to now charge that same fool with vandalism or trespassing reeks of double jeopardy.

While the courts used St. Paul, MN to strike down a ban on speech, the court has ruled that people who commit 'hate crimes' motivated by bigotry may be sentenced to extra punishment *without violating their free-speech rights* (emphasis added). In essence, you can say what you want, but not while committing a crime! This is the legislation of morality by instituting extra punishment to the 'immoral.'

As Afro-American, women and gay groups scrambled to support such legislation, they assumed that they were somehow above reproach due to their status as the oppressed. However, hate crime legislation is being applied to Afro-Americans, artists, and the poor with a fervor that is frightening. Nineteen-year-old Todd Mitchell, who is black, received a double sentence for inciting the beating of a 14-year-old white youth. The ordinance he was convicted under permits longer prison terms for crimes motivated by racial or other bias. So, what has our fellow learned? The next time you beat whitey, just beat him — don't say a damn thing to him! This is not a viable solution to racial antagonisms.

When Paul Broussard, a 27-year-old gay man, was violently clubbed to death by a group of teenagers, gay activists convinced Houston police to develop a special undercover unit to patrol the city's gay areas for awhile. The officers of the unit admitted they were shocked at the level of violence against gays. These officers would not have so shocked had they taken the pleas of the gay community seriously. Lack of legal recourse means it's okay to beat up on gay people. This is not equal protection under the law. It is not okay to beat up on anyone, regardless of the particular community in which they belong. Hate crime legislation actually buys into the system of thought that equates difference with inferiority in the grand scheme of American jurisprudence. This paternalistic and fascistic ideology will only exacerbate the social tensions in our society.

To tell the truth, I am sick and tired of being a pawn for the liberal establishment's whims — I want equality under the law and I want it now! I don't want some high-faluting, legal mumbo-jumbo that requires people to call me a nigger dyke while they kick my ass before I can get some justice. What I need are honest officers who can see my humanity and realize an assault is an assault regardless of my association with any social group. What I need is a judicial system that will not use my status as a reason to assume that I do not deserve justice.

Barbara Beebe is a freelance writer residing in Fayetteville, NC. She has a B.S. in Criminal Justice.

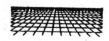

TAX THIS, PAL!

John Longhi

Death and Taxes. At times the two can seem equally pernicious, equally mysterious in their random allotments of misfortune. Take the strange case of Paul Mavrides. Mavrides is co-creator of everyone's favorite potheads, the Freak Brothers. His demon pen has also spat out much of the twisted mirth and images associated with J. R. Bob Dobbs and the Church of the Subgenius. Now Mavrides finds himself in a nightmarish situation with the Sales Tax Equalization Board of California that borders on Kafka-esque. Basically they want to charge sales tax on his royalties. The Boards case revolves around an interpretation of Regulation 1543 of the current Sales and Use Regulation Code. This is where things begin to get ugly.

The whole case depends on the state classifying comics art as a specific kind of object. They are zeroing in on the artwork in its camera-ready form, trying to classify it as a special printing aid and not as a manuscript. Under these guidelines the comic work becomes commercial art and not literature. It is ironic that the state of California waited until after Art Spiegelman's *Maus* won the Pulitzer Prize to reclassify comics. This seems like a slap in the face to all the comic artists who have struggled for decades to bring legitimate recognition to the field. But the brass tacks of this case are probably more simple than the big questions of what is or isn't art. The state of California is broke and suffering from one of the worst recessions in its history. Not even ru-

mors of a recovery run through the once golden state. A reward system exists for bureaucrats who can come up with novel forms of revenue. If there is a settlement the person who blew the whistle on the delinquent offender can get a cut of the cash. The state of California will take whatever they can from whoever they can get it from. So are they out to get underground comics? Because of Paul's affiliation with the Church of the Subgenius one cant help but ask, Is there a conspiracy?

No, according to Mavrides. They didn't go after any kind of publishing, or any kind of comic in particular, Paul told me recently. I've never been led to suspect, even in my wildest moments of paranoia that somebody didn't like my work and decided to do this to *me*. He feels that he was picked at random, swept up in the states ceaseless search for revenue.

Mavrides first came to the states attention in 1991 when a mistake in their records erroneously attributed him with an extra $80,000 more than he actually made. After a year and a half of wrangling he finally managed to get that straightened out. But Mavrides barely had time to breathe a sigh of relief before the Board of Equalization began to reinterpret an old law on the books in an attempt to get more money from him.

One has to ask, Why? The profits from alternative and underground comics are marginal at best. Few artists make their living at it and those that do usually just squeak by. The total revenues generated by Last

Gasp or Rip Off Press are laughable compared to the mega-bucks one ish of Spidey makes. But Mavrides sees a method to their madness. Even bottom feeders go through an evolutionary progression. The State Tax Board may just be working its way up the food chain.

They said to themselves, How do these rules we already have apply to this cartoonist? Paul explained. You can set a precedent with the application of regulations. The Board doesn't make these laws, the Legislature writes these regulations, it puts them into the sales tax code that the Board follows. The Board is allowed to interpret these regulations. And this is a grey area. So the Board is interpreting the regulations in its favor. There's no clearly spelled out rule on what this type of literature consists of. The Boards interpreting it a certain way, if I were to comply then they'd have a precedent of compliance. A couple more people at my level and they're starting to rack up a record, like people are agreeing and going along with our interpretation as correct. This gives their interpretation more weight when they decide to go after Image comics. [*Now you're talking some bucks* - JL] It makes it that much more difficult for Image who could defend themselves without having to resort to aid from the Comics Defense Fund. It would make their [Images] battle against this that much more difficult because the Board already has people in compliance. If the Board had showed up with a bill for like ten bucks, I might not have concerned myself with it so much as to think through what was going on.

But the Board didn't show up with a bill for ten bucks. They want around two grand. That's enough to buy a car, a years worth of groceries, or one hell of a bag of pot. The taxman starts at the bottom and works his way to the top.

That wasn't necessarily their plan but that's the process, Paul continued. I don't know if there's some strategy behind this. But my resistance has made them have to consider defending their position.

Mavrides has had to engage legal council, and start working his way through the official appeals process. With support from the Comic Book Legal Defense Fund he is ready to spend ten to fifteen times the contested amount to overturn the Boards judgement.

If established as a precedent the Boards ruling could have a chilling effect on the comics industry, especially in the state of California. The increased accounting and administrative costs to small and independent comics publishers and artists could put them out of business. Most of these companies survive on a shoestring already. Mavrides feels the new taxes could cause many publishers to close up shop and leave the state.

Ron Turner, publisher of Last Gasp comics feels the states moves effectively adds up to a double tax. The consumer already has to pay sales tax on a comic when they buy it in a store. If publishers have to also pay tax on the original artwork, then the Tax Board is taking from both ends. If we had to pay tax on our artwork right when we got it in, then we would definitely have to raise the price of the item were selling, Turner said. And then it would seem that if the consumer were paying tax at the end, then they're really paying a double tax. I thought that was illegal. According to Turner, a rough ratio would be that every extra nickel's worth of production costs would lead to an extra quarters worth of cover price for the consumer.

The prospects of profit as an underground cartoonist are already pretty grim. The burden of extra

COMIC BOOKS!

THE BASTARD CHILD OF ART AND LITERATURE, COMMONLY MISHELD TO BE A DIVERSION FOR KIDS AND IDIOTS, THE COMIC BOOK'S ORIGINS PREDATE THE *WRITTEN WORD*...

STORIES TO STUN A ROTTING BRAIN COMICS

by PAUL MAVRIDES ©1993

30,000 BC. A DAMP, DARK CAVE IN SPAIN AND THE BIRTH OF LITERATURE!

THAT'S NOT HOW I REMEMBER IT!

THE INVENTION OF HIEROGLYPHS AND PICTO-GLYPHS REFINES THE RELATIONSHIP BETWEEN STORYTELLING, ART AND WRITING...

ART, THEN, HAS AN INHERENT ABILITY TO CONVEY INFORMATION AND *TELL STORIES* — WHEN USED SEQUENTIALLY, ART CAN FUNCTION AS A FORM OF LITERATURE.

PERHAPS MANY OF HISTORY'S GREATEST AUTHORS USED PROSE EXCLUSIVELY SIMPLY BECAUSE THEY WERE SUCH LOUSY ARTISTS...

Call me Ishmael.

THE MODERN COMIC BOOK IS A COMBINATION OF WRITING *AND* ARTWORK WHOSE GESTALT CREATES A *LITERARY WORK*, GOOD *OR* BAD. ONE CANNOT DISPUTE TASTE.

REALLY, ONE NEEDN'T USE WORDS **AT ALL** TO WRITE WITH PICTURES...

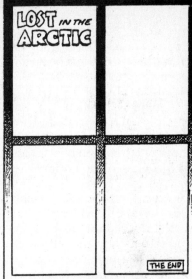

LOST *IN THE* ARCTIC

THE END

... OR, FOR THAT MATTER, USE EVEN *PICTURES THEMSELVES!* THE TOPOLOGICAL INFORMATIONAL NATURE OF THE COMIC PAGE ALLOWS FOR ALMOST INFINITE VARIATION...

OF COURSE, *SOME* CLAIM THAT COMIC BOOK DRAWINGS ARE NOTHING BUT "COMMERCIAL ART."

A DRAWING IS AN *ILLUSTRATION,* AND AN ILLUSTRATION CAN'T BE AN AUTHOR'S MANUSCRIPT ACCORDING TO CALIFORNIA STATE SALES TAX REGULATION 1543 (b)(3)(B)(5), THEREFORE *COMIC BOOK CREATORS* ARE **NOT** *AUTHORS* AND DO NOT SHARE THE RIGHTS AND EXEMPTIONS OF AUTHORS.

'NUFF SAID.

TOSS

MAUS

10

ART SPIEGELMAN'S COMIC BOOK, MAUS, WON A PULITZER PRIZE AND A GUGGENHEIM FELLOWSHIP.

THAT TYPE OF BUREAUCRATIC LOGIC ILL SERVES FREEDOM OF SPEECH WHEN ITS SOLE JUSTIFICATION IS MERELY TO RAISE TAX REVENUES.

BOMBS AWAY!

10 TONS OF TAX

10

SO CARTOONISTS AREN'T AUTHORS. LIKE, BIG DEAL. WHAT DIFFERENCE COULD IT MAKE ANYWAY?

NEXT: THE CARTOONISTS STRIKE BACK!

taxes might drive even more people away from the comics field. In effect, Mavrides feels this limits artists' rights to free speech. If it is made too difficult for one to express oneself in a certain medium, doesn't that effectively equate to censorship? The same standard could be applied to ridiculous lengths. Under its guidelines any form of visually-rendered manuscript could be deemed commercial art and taxed, regardless of its literary content.

Its really not their place to make decisions like this, Mavrides said. The Board suddenly has the power to decide who's an author and who's not. I don't think they intended to do that. I don't think they thought it through. They might not have done this at all if they had thought through this.

What do you do in the case of William Blake and his poetry? Where Blake hand wrote poems and illustrated them, and specifically instructed that they were not to be reproduced in any other form? Some California publisher puts out a book of his. Now Blake's work is in the public domain but if he was still alive, because of the nature of this the Board conceivably might suddenly declare that Blake was not an author.

Turner agrees. Underneath this, of course, is the more serious thing to me, he said. Once again these people have failed to recognize that cartoon art, comics, is perhaps the most literate of the arts. By taking this stance they are putting down the idea of comics. They're not understanding that this is not just a child's thing. We have some people who, in their desperation for making money or maybe keeping their jobs, are willing to walk all over the rights and the definition of the English language.

So far, this issue has only arisen in California. But Mavrides fears it could be applied as a national prece-

dent if the guidelines turn out to be profitable. Legally, California is often a trailblazer for other states. If New York state adopted these sales tax rules Art Spiegelman's Maus would be deemed commercial art and he would have to pay extra. Not even a Pulitzer stands in the way of the taxman.

A lot of the states argument depends on assigning comic art a particular form. A legally recognized shape that is taxable.

Basically the states saying my original comics pages aren't an authors manuscript, Mavrides said. Because one takes a copy camera stat of them and that's directly used to make a negative for reproduction. Therefore, rather than being a manuscript this is only a printers aid. Because when an author turns in a manuscript its typed, its on a computer disk, or its in some form that doesn't get direct reproduction. Now that seems like a very false argument to me because you have the case I already mentioned where you have a handwritten manuscript and that is directly reproduced. I was given the reason that the topical nature of the prose information on the page overrides the characters as a graphic and therefore it is still an authors manuscript. I pointed out that I can write a story with pictures, without using words. And the topical information nature of that process makes it just as valid as a chunk of written prose.

A whole new dimension of ambiguity opens up when one considers computers. Many works of art and even some comics are created on disk these days and their only form is as electronic impulses. Many of the graphics one sees in magazines such as Mondo 2000 never actually exist in hard copy. They often go direct from disk to printed color separations and an actual artifact never exists. If a comic was made on a computer the states argument breaks down. But Mavrides is pessimistic. He feels its just a matter of time before they tax computer-generated comics and art-work as well.

They're at a loss there, he said. Regulations are in a rush to keep up. Nobody wrote a regulation covering CD-ROMs specifically, so until they do they have to figure out what it is. With computer technologies they're working on regulations to tax them, but they cant keep up. Every time you turn around there's a new way of transferring information.

But as soon as they figure out what it is they'll find a way to get money out of it.

I could be drawing these comics on the sides of dogs and cats and turning them into the publisher, Mavrides adds. It really doesn't mat-ter, this whole physical object of my manuscript issue is really beside the point as far as I'm concerned. I think they never applied any of these rules to comics before. I have the impres-sion that nobody at the Board is really familiar with comics as a literary form. Its not their place to make de-cisions like this.

Mavrides has not broken any laws. The situation he finds himself in has never happened to anyone be-fore. He has the bad luck of being an example case. Of being the first in his field that the state has decided to put a squeeze on.

Excerpts from Paul Mavrides' comics, **Cover-up Lowdown,** *dealing with the assassination of John F. Kennedy can be found in this issue of* **Gauntlet** *(Re-printed with permission from* **Cover-Up Lowdown,** *published by Rip Off Press Inc., 1977). John Longhi is the author of a book of short stories* **Bricks and An-chors** *and his forthcoming collection,* **Rise and Fall of Third Leg,** *will have a cover by R. Crumb.*

"BOILED" DIANA

Scott Cunningham

Underground. publications, by definition, touch on topics of transgressions whether it be sexual, political, philosophical or artistic. Often it's a blend of all four. The "self" in self-publishing is the ying to the yang of "self"-censorship. Self-publishing is the only way to guaran-tee complete control over your own material. By putting out your own 'zine you can beat the inherent checks and balances built into com-mercial driven mainstream publica-tions. And now with the rise of "political correctness" one more nail goes into the coffin of free speech. Almost everyone who does self-pub-lish loses money and wastes valuable T.V.-watching time; their measly re-wards coming in occasional fan let-ters or positive reviews in other 'zines. So imagine the hell of going through tedious production work to grind out your occasional effort, and your prize is jail time. It could happen in the case of Mike Diana, poor white trash from the Sunshine State, who's little digest of comics and stories may wind him behind bars.

Mike Diana works at his dads convenience store in Largo, Fl., sell-ing cigarettes and beer to the drunks and crackheads who wander into the place looking like wasted cannibals from the gory zombie movies he loves. Until recently, he used to go home to the trailer he lived in with his younger brother and draw comics every night. But when the news of his indictment hit the papers, there was some problems with the police and the people who were letting him stay there asked him to leave. Mike's a twenty-two year old artist and an enemy of the state — at least the state of Florida. And I guess that means I am too, since I've contributed work to his magazine ever since I met him — through the mail — in 1989, crating a show on 'zines. There were hundreds of publications in the exhibit, lots of them exploring sexually deviate themes; but somehow Mike's comic *Angel Fuck* (now renamed *Boiled Angel* because of trouble with the Post Office over the f-word in the title) remained the strongest in my memory, simply because it was so extreme. It's as if all the evil and nasty images vomited forth by underground '60s id —monsters like Rory Hayes and S. Clay Wilson had been concentrated and combined with the pop violence of contemporary gore movies and the minimal lyrics of hardcore punk music. Drawn in a primitive style of glorified high school doodles, Mike's work had an obsessive urgency that undercut its cynical, flat humor. A typical Mike Diana story starts with a young boy excited to hear he's finally been adopted, then immediately being beaten and raped by his new father once they get alone. The boy winds up slaving away at his evil dad's factory, grinding up babies for dog food. He eventually kills daddy, but the abuse doesn't stop there. The boy's dog ends up raping him. ("Oh no, Spot, not you too!")

In the land of the free and the home of the brave, Mike has managed to cross the line again and again. His work dealing with child abuse, sex. murder, torture and satanism has, over the years I've known him, turned *Boiled Angel* into a magnet of controversy. Whenever comic shops get raided *Boiled Angel* always heads the list of obscene materials confiscated. in 1990, Mike became a suspect in the FBI's investigation into a Gainsville serial killer *simply because of the material he was printing* — no other evidence was necessary for the Bureau to question him and request a blood test. Recently Last Gasp one of the biggest alternative distributors around, refused to reorder *Run Ron* a successful selling title, because Mike's strip had drawn such strong complaints (though Tower Books should be commended for continuing to sell *Run Ron* and *Boiled Angel*). When you think about it, the Florida indictment seemed destined though it's strange it would come down now, since it's been over a year-and-a-half ago that the last issue of *Boiled Angel* appeared.

But then who can figure Florida, anyway? The same state that brought you the 2 Live Crew trial now has decided to boost Mike's career by

GET A PRIZE IN EVERY BOX OF JESUS FREAKS CERIAL!! MCD '91

YUM!

SIMON HELPS JESUS

JESUS FALLS THE SECOND TIME

ACK!

Forgive me!

JESUS FREAKS

JESUS FALLS THE THIRD TIME

JESUS DIES ON THE CROSS

attacking his first amendment rights. And there may be no escape from Florida's moralistic goosestep, now that Dade County's own Janet Reno is calling the shots for the whole country. An eye-popping story about what a secret right-wing nutcase she really is was exposed by Alexander Cockburn's in his column for *The Nation* in April, 1993. He recounts her trumped up case against a fifteen-year-old boy accused of child molestation, revealing her demonization of a totally innocent kid. After reading that article, I couldn't help thinking about Reno's move to attack the Davidian Complex because of rumors of child abuse (*still* just rumors, I might point out) and you can see a pattern: as soon as there's a whiff of possible child abuse, individual rights literally go up in smoke. Reno's motto, "We had to kill the children to save them" may become this country's idea of justice for the next few years.

Florida's Assistant State Attorney Stuart Baggish states: "The First Amendment was framed and built for the benefit of society. It was never

contemplated for the protection of obscene materials the contents of which weaken the moral fiber of society. That's why we'll be asking for jail time—the maximum punishment." If found guilty of the three misdemeanor charges for producing lewd and obscene material, Mike could be sentenced to three years in jail and fined $3000. His case has been taken up by the Comics Legal Defense Fund, and his trial date is due to be set during a hearing before a judge in late-July. If you want to write Mike in support, or beg him for copies of the infamous issues 7 and 8 of *Boiled Angel* —now state's evidence in the case — he can be contacted at: P.O. Box 5254, Largo, Fl. 34649. To see his most recent work available, check out Issue #19 of *World War 3 Illustrated*, Issue #3 of *Snake Eyes* and Issue 8 of *The Brutarian*.

Chelsea Quinn Yarbro, *Chairman of the Board of Trustees of Horror Writers of America, is a truly prolific writer. She has sold 49 books, at least 35 of which are novels. However, to date she has not been able to place Magnificat, which is strange considering her track record. As a matter of fact, in the last 25 years, once she has completed a manuscript she has always found a home for it. Her most recent novel, Darker Jewels, was published by Tor in 1993. So what makes Magnificat different? For the record, the book has been turned down by a number of publishers due to its length — 220,000 words. Off the record, however, one editor has told her she'd been instructed by her superior not to buy anything that would offend the Catholic Church, as this would very clearly do. Four other editors, according to Yarbro, have made similar intimations. "I must assume that the Archdiocese of New York has the publishing world running scared," she concludes. Her favorite rejection, so far, she says "was from an editor who found it confusing to have all the members of the College of Cardinals called Cardinal, and couldn't I call some of them something else?" Whether Magnificat sees publication remains to be seen, but what follows is the first chapter which gives the reader a good idea what may be causing the fuss.*

Magnificat

Chelsea Quinn Yarbro

Chapter 1

As he set the nib of his pen on the vellum, Ottone, Cardinal Folgar was possessed by a strange dizziness; there was a whiteness behind his eyes, light that was more than light, a fluttering of breath, a sense that something hovered over him, a moment that was suspended in eternity. Then it was gone and he passed a shaking hand across his brow, murmuring thanks to God that He had chosen to leave him on earth a little longer. How ironic, he thought in the next instant as he touched the crucifix that hung on his breast, if he died now, while the Cardinals were gathered in conclave to choose a new Pope: a new Pope for the second time in three years, and with the millennium fast approaching, bringing with it a religious fervor Cardinal Folgar had not encountered before in his lifetime.

From inclination as much as habit the Cardinal still prayed in Latin, relishing the tolling cadences he had mastered as a child. Now the familiar liturgy took his mind off the peculiar, brief episode that might presage disaster. His brother had died of a stroke,

just three years ago. Perhaps this was how it had begun. He continued his thanks to God, shutting out the arthritic ache in his knees as well as his growing irritation with his fellow-Princes of the Church, who, like him, were about to submit their ballots to be counted. He set aside the old-fashioned crow-quill pen.

Then he glanced down at the vellum and shook his head. He had been instructed to disguise his handwriting, and certainly succeeded in doing so. Would it be possible to read the name of Sylvestre, Cardinal Jung in that disjointed scrawl? That was not supposed to be his concern. He crossed himself and got up from his knees, impatient to be done. There was another long week of manoeuvering, he was convinced, before his own conservative faction and Marc-Luc, Cardinal Gemme's radicals would come to terms. Both sides would probably compromise, either with the popular Vitale, Cardinal Cadini, or the Canadian, Dominique, Cardinal Hetre. For the time being, there was a ritual to the politics of the conclave as there was to everything in the Church — hence his temporary support of Cardinal Jung, though he did not want the pompous Swiss to be elected.

He put his vellum into a foil-lined envelope and began to heat sealing wax over a match. This was one reform of John-Paul II's he could approve, this simplifying of the presentation of ballots; as he pressed his Cardinal's ring into the dollop of hot wax, he thought he felt a distant, fleeting echo of his earlier disorientation. He blew out the match and resumed his prayers.

✦   ✦

Not far from Cardinal Folgar's conclave cell, Jivin, Cardinal Tayibha completed his prayers without finding the peace he sought. He had heard that the conclaves were more politics than religion, but he had not anticipated how extreme it would be, with the liberal and conservative elements of the Church so acrimoniously divided. He had attempted to conceal his shock and dismay but knew he had failed. As the newest Cardinal, he was the least prepared for what he encountered here; he almost regretted the knowledge he had acquired in the last thirteen days as the Cardinals feinted and reposited for advantage. How far he had come from the simple faith of his youth, the trust of his ordination. At fifty-one he was becoming a skeptic.

It was time to vote, he knew, and he could not think of any name to put on the vellum. The last time he had voted for Felipe, Cardinal Pingari, as a gesture of support for the Filipino, but knew that a second such endorsement would be wasted: Cardinal Pingari himself had asked that he not be considered. He admired Vincent, Cardinal Walgren of Los Angeles, who had accomplished such wonders with youth gangs and drug dealers. But was that acumen enough to recommend him for the Papacy? And how would the world respond to an American Pope?

He was not aware that he had taken his pen in hand and marked the vellum. It must be the fatigue, he decided as he peered at the scratchings. He had been staying up nights for meditation and prayers; during the day he fasted. Now those disciplines were taking their toll. The writing looked like doodles, he thought, or Chinese. He reached for his foil-lined envelope and prepared to seal his vote, wondering distantly whose name he had written.

✦   ✦

When Marc-Luc, Cardinal Gemme handed over his sealed ballot, he left his cell for Vespers, ready to hear the tally of the votes as soon as the service was concluded. He could not conceal the aggravation that consumed him as he walked down the Sistine Chapel, ignoring Michelangelo's splendor overhead. If only Urban IX had lived another year! There would have been time to organize the Church liberals against the forces of conservatism which were gaining strength in the Church as the Third Millennium approached. It was hard to believe. In just three years the Third Millennium would begin, and the Church was in as much disarray as the rest of Christianity in anticipating 2001 A. D. Every extremist group was preaching chaos and the Second Coming, and the conservatives in the Church sympathized with this madness. Without the sweeping changes of John-Paul II in the last decade, the Church would be even more hampered than it had become; at least there was a mechanism for change and reform, little as it was used. Inwardly he was afraid that it was too late, for the Cardinals with Cardinal Folgar were entrenched and prepared to resist to the last. As it was, he had tried to rally the Europeans along with the Third World Cardinals to stand against the reactionaries. The longer it took to elect the Pope, the more he feared the outcome of the conclave.

His own vote puzzled him, for he had been distracted when he wrote the name of his candidate. It was an effort to make sense of the marks on the vellum, but he supposed that the secretaries were used to that and would make allowances for his attempts to disguise his hand. He stopped walking as he chided himself for his worldliness; the Apostolic Succession, he reminded himself sternly, was the result of the visitation of the Holy Spirit, not the result of Vatican skulduggery. That, above all, must be maintained or the whole fabric of Catholicism unraveled. Very carefully he crossed himself and tried to turn his thoughts to more spiritual paths. As he strove to keep his mind away from politics, he heard the opening words of Vespers — today in German — and he hastened to join the other Cardinals in worship.

✦ ✦

It was Vitale, Cardinal Cadini who spoke for all of them when the secretary presented himself to them fully two hours after he was expected. "What is the trouble, Father?" He broke with tradition in asking the question, but Cardinal Cadini had made a career of breaking tradition since as a young Monsignor he had been an aide to John XXIII, and no one was shocked by him now. "Tell us."

The secretary, grown old at the Vatican, and seeming to be made of the same parchment as were many of the documents he tended, offered a gesture of apology. "Yes, Eminences," he said, his voice almost breaking. "I fear there may be a . . . a problem."

"Well, what is it?" demanded Sylvestre, Cardinal Jung, his corpulent, satin-clad body as polished as a Dresden figurine. "Tell us at once."

Father McEllton blinked in helplessness. "It is not my sin, Eminences. I am not in error. I thought at first I was, but when all the ballots were examined . . . I have done nothing to be ashamed of, but I must ask you to pardon me."

"Certainly," said Cardinal Cadini, his raisin eyes twinkling. "We will all pardon you, every one of us, Father McEllton, if only you will tell us what is wrong."

There was a murmur of consent from the eighty-nine Cardinals, and one or two mutters at the delay.

"Have we a Pope or not?" Cardinal Folgar asked emphatically.

"Eminences, we have . . . consensus." He turned pale. "You have all written the same name.

"All of us?" Cardinal Folgar was dumbfounded that all the Cardinals would support Cardinal Jung.

A susurrus passed through the men gathered around Father McEllton, and one or two of the Princes of the Church crossed themselves.

"How is that possible?" asked Cardinal Pingari with a polite nod to the cadaverous Cardinal Lepescu at his side. Both men wore dignity more prominently than their red cassocks.

"If we truly have consensus," said the doubtful Dominique, Cardinal Hetre, "then why have we not followed procedure?" He was a stickler for procedure, always.

Once again Father McEllton dithered. "You see, I didn't understand at first. I did not see. How could I? What would lead me to think . . . I thought it was the handwriting." He wrung his fingers as if to force the offending words out of them. "I ask your pardon, Eminences. I mean no disrespect. If Father Zirhendakru had not been . . . as it was, he identified the . . . the name."

"Surely our handwriting was not that bad," suggested the older Polish Cardinal, his eyes hard and bright in his wrinkled face. He had supported the controversial Tokuyu, Cardinal Tsukamara, and flatly refused to suppose that all the rest of the College of Cardinals did as well. If only he had paid more attention to how he wrote the name of his ballot; but he had been momen-

Harry O. Morris

tarily distracted when he put his pen to the vellum, an inexcusable lapse.

"It was . . . it was all the same," said Father McEllton at last. "All the same name."

"And who is it?" the senior Cardinal from Brazil asked bluntly, glowering at Father McEllton. "What is it that distresses you?" Beside him, Jaime, Cardinal O'Higgins of Mexico City scowled portentously, the expression incongruous in his impish face.

"We ought not to receive the information you have for us this way, no matter what the awkwardness of it may be," said Cardinal Tayibha. "There is ritual — "

"It is not the name of anyone here," blurted out Father McEllton. Now that he had spoken the dreadful news, he felt suddenly, maddeningly calm. Nothing else would be as appalling as telling them that.

"What do you mean, it isn't the name of anyone here?" Cardinal Folgar said in disbelieving indignation. Which of the three celebrated Archbishops had been able to gain the Papacy when they had not yet achieved their red hats? How could there be unanimity, when he himself had not supported any of the Archbishops? Cardinal Folgar began to review all those Cardinals who might be expected to show support for one of the three famous Archbishops, but could not fathom how such a thing could happen, certainly not unanimously. "There has been a mistake," he said, and saw that most of the Cardinals agreed with him.

"Yes, precisely. It is a mistake, one that requires correction.

The name . . . it is . . . it is the name of a foreigner." Father McEllton folded his hands. "It is not the name I recognize, nor does the computer." He stared straight ahead. "We have gone through all the registers and we have not found the name."

This time a third of the Cardinals crossed themselves and the words that were whispered among them were less indignant than before. One or two of the Cardinals appeared almost frightened.

"But you say Father Zirhendakru recognized it," prompted Cardinal Hetre, as much to stave off further distress as to obtain the offending name. These delays were making his headache worse.

"Not precisely. He knew the language, and he translated it." Father McEllton had turned bright red, his fair skin taking his blush like a stain.

"Tell us, Father," said Cardinal Cadini with his world-famous smile. "What is the name. Who have we all endorsed?" The smile grew broader, so that everyone would be certain he was joking, not commanding.

"It . . . " He took a deep breath, feeling his heart slamming in his chest. If only Our Lady would protect him through this ordeal, he would retire from Vatican service for the rest of his life and devote it to study and assisting the poor, he vowed. "It is Zhu . . . Zhuang Renxin, or so father Zirhendakru tells me." He stumbled over the word, unable to pronounce the inflections.

The Cardinals were silent.

Then Cardinal Folgar spoke for all of them, shaking with the intensity of his emotions. "What nonsense is this?"

Immediately the other Cardinals added their questions and demands. The noise grew tremendous.

"That is what Father Zirhendakru says," Father McEllton repeated several times, unable to think of anything else to offer them. He had no explanation at all.

Finally Cardinal Hetre managed to make himself heard over the rest of them. "It is obviously a prank," he said, choosing the least inflammatory word he could think of. "Someone is trying to influence the conclave or make mock of it without direct interference."

This brought nods of agreement and a few condemning outbursts, including one staunch defense of Vatican Security. The growing awe that had possessed the Cardinals now vanished and was replaced by outrange.

"It had to be the Communists," said Cardinal Jung at once, certain that they would want to sew dissention in the ranks, and if the name on the ballot was Chinese, it only served to prove his point. "They want to destroy the Church, and they want to promote their Godless cause in the eyes of the world. What better way than this?"

"It has to be the Separatists," corrected Michon, Cardinal Belleau, referring to the group of excommunicated priests and nuns who had splintered from the Church and now had established their own Vatican and Pope on the other side of Rome near Settecamini, acting in open defiance of the Holy See.

"Incredible," murmured Cardinal Cadini, for once unable to come up with a single witty remark.

"It is obvious that we are being duped," said Ectore, Cardinal Fiorivi, the most respected legal mind in the highest ranks of the Church and currently Vatican Secretary of State. "Someone, and it does not matter who, is attempting to impugn our credibility, to cast doubt on any Pope we elect. It is up to us to use our best judgment now and not permit this incident to interfere with our task here. His voice, resonant and deep as a fine bell, quieted the gathering. "It behooves us to withdraw for meditation and prayer tonight, and in the morning we will have to discuss what we wish to do with these ballots. We will have to find a way to keep this information from reaching the public; it will be difficult, because whoever is responsible will certainly do their best to inform all the news media of what has happened, if only to put forward embarrassing questions. We must not permit this to occur, and we will need to counteract the rumors as soon as possible. In the meantime, you, Father McEllton, will announce that we have given the day to discussion and prayer and have not cast votes this evening, to forestall another deadlock. Perhaps our reticence will cause the ones responsible to show themselves."

There were a few words of agreement at Cardinal Fiorivi's proposals, but Cardinal Tayibha could not go along with the others.

"Eminences," he said, his voice cracking, "we are here to

invite the Holy Spirit to make itself known to us. We have all written a name, the same name. Might not this be a manifestation of the Holy Spirit? It is said that the Holy Spirit could inspire us to elect any living soul on the earth to occupy the Throne of Saint Peter. Dare we presume to declare ourselves above the visitation of the Holy Spirit, and the true Will of God if that is what has actually occurred?"

"The Holy Spirit would not be a recommending a Chinese to be Pope," announced Cardinal Folgar. "It's absurd to think otherwise. We know the dogma, but we know the Church, as well." His smile was condescending as he went on to the soft-spoken Cardinal from Madras. "It is your first time in conclave, and you are still learning your way. Your piety does you credit, of course, but in circumstances like this, it is essential that we do not permit ourselves to be deceived. So many Catholics are gullible and can be taken in by any number of ruses, and never more so than when we are in conclave." He looked around and saw favorable responses in the eyes of many of the Cardinals. "We have been the victims of a clever, evil joke, and we must be at pains to guard against similar incidents."

Again there were gestures of support, a few quite emphatic.

But Hunfredo, Cardinal Montebranco was not convinced. "How can you assume that we have been deceived? Is it impossible that the Holy Spirit would touch each of us, if God wished it?"

"We pray that we will receive the gifts of the Holy Spirit," said Cardinal Jung at once, "but Folgar is right; it is not credible that the Holy Spirit would offer the name of a Chinese." He had a deep, plumy laugh. "How could such a thing happen?"

"If it is the Will of God," said the venerable Cardinal Montebranco, "it would require only to exist; credibility is for fallible humans." He crossed himself. "I pray that we are not like Peter, to deny Our Lord when He is present."

"Do you seriously suppose that the Holy Spirit would offer the name of a Chinese? A non-Catholic? A Communist?" demanded Cardinal Jung, his voice rising in pitch with each question.

"No," said Cardinal O'Higgins in a thoughtful voice. "No, but that does not mean anything when dealing with matters of God. What we suppose is as nothing." He glanced nervously over his shoulder. "It would be easier to turn away if only a few had written the name, but as we all did, it is . . . "

"Proof that the saboteurs have agents in the Vatican, as we have long suspected," said Cardinal Folgar promptly. "This is the result of careful planning, that may have taken years to put into action. Whatever their goals and whoever they are, they have overstepped themselves here. That shows pride, and their error. Had they given the . . . vision to half our number, it would appear odd but reasonable, but they become greedy, and that was the source of their failure." He motioned to Father McEllton. "You have done well by coming to us in this way. If you had spoken officially we would have had to make a state-

Harry O. Morris

ment and we can say nothing official about this. When we reveal tomorrow that we have not yet reached a decision, we will know our enemies by their responses." He crossed himself and folded his hands, looking very placid. "It might be best if we retire at once, so that we can explore our thoughts in privacy; we will give nothing away to our enemies if we are silent."

Cardinal Shumwoe nodded gravely, his densely black skin making him look like a walking shadow. "In the morning we must discuss our experiences. Until then, I am convinced Cardinal Folgar is right — the less we are together the less chance there is that we will weaken our position." To provide an example he turned away and started toward his temporary cell.

"It is well-advised," said Cardinal Hetre, indicating the other Canadian Cardinal, Victor, Cardinal Mnientek. "Come, Eminence."

"For Canada?" asked Cardinal Mnientek with a lift to his brows; the mischief in his eyes was at odds with his angular Polish features.

"For the memory of Urban IX, and for the benefit of the Church," said Cardinal Hetre.. "We owe that much to his reign, surely; we all do," he added pointedly.

Several Cardinals agreed, a few of them moving away with the two Canadians; others were confused by this failure of protocol and uncertain of what was best to do.

Several Cardinals agreed, a few of them moving away with the two Canadians; others were confused by this failure of protocol and uncertain of what was best to do.

Charles, Cardinal Mendosa took up the case, standing as if he were about to get on a half-broke horse. "The less we say about this, the better. I'm not suggesting we should ignore it — nothing like that. But we need to have our priorities straight. After we have a Pope, then we can set about finding out what this thing was and who was behind it. In the meantime, I thought we better get a new kitchen staff while we're in here. Something got hold of us, and if it wasn't the Holy Spirit, it was probably in the air or the food. Those are the two things we all share. So we'll start with the food: it's easier." He had one hand on his hip as if there might be a phantom six-gun under his fingers. "And when we find out who's doing this, we'd best deal with them quickly and quietly. We don't want any publicity getting out about this. You know the press would be all over us, and they're bad enough as it is with every Bible-thumping preaching from one end of the world to the other talking about a Second Coming and the Antichrist." He crossed himself. "God is better served without a lot of glitz and glamour."

It galled Cardinal Folgar to agree with the tall, rangy Texan from Houston, but he knew it was the wisest course. "We are all aware it would be ill-advised for the world to learn of this."

"Might give them ideas," added Cardinal Mendosa. "They could take a notion to question everything, to think it's all conspiracies. It's bad enough watching the loonies on TV talking about the Second Coming as if it were a rock concert. I see a lot of that back home."

Cardinal Folgar stifled the retort he longed to give about Americans in general and Texans in particular; instead he said, "We must think of the Church, how it is to endure the next three years, until we are safely launched on the new millennium."

Cardinal van Hooven peered out through the pebble-thick lenses of his steel-rimmed spectacles. "Silence, Eminences. Silence first. Leave a little time for the soul to speak. We've already said too much, and confounded our minds. We must quiet the disorder within ourselves and turn our thoughts to the inner light where God is found." He leaned on his cane as he made his way toward his temporary cell, saying as he went, "I will retire for the evening. You may concoct whatever tale you wish to placate the press."

"He has the right idea," said Cardinal Mendosa. "Let's just make sure that Father McEllton doesn't end up with egg on his face, all right?" He looked around. "Okay. You: Gemme. You're the one the press likes best. You can work out the right way to explain what's going on in here, without telling them much. Make sure the reporters don't spook you." He touched his pectoral crucifix and his weathered face softened. "We owe it to the Church, Gemme."

"Of course," said Cardinal Gemme harshly.

"We're depending on you." Cardinal Mendosa grinned at Cardinal Gemme. "I'll make special mention of you in my prayers, Eminence."

Cardinal Gemme swung around and stalked away from the small remaining knot of Cardinals.

✦ ✦

It was well into the night when Jivin, Cardinal Tayibha finally ceased his meditations. For the last two hours he had permitted himself to hope that the disastrous ballots were an isolated incident, something they had faced and defeated; now he wanted a little rest before the Cardinals met again. He thought of God, the mystery of Him, and for once was chilled instead of comforted. He rose from his knees and prepared himself for bed, hoping that the fragile serenity he had found for himself would sustain him into the morning when he would need it most.

As he slipped between the sheets, he had one last frison of doubt: what if they were opposing the Will of God? What if that Chinese name was truly the mandate of the Holy Spirit, and not some clever psychological manipulation on the part of those seeking to sabotage the conclave and the Church? He recalled that anyone elected twice by the College of Cardinals could not refuse the Papacy; the Cardinals could not elect another Pope until thee one elected twice had served. He shuddered as he closed his eyes.

With an effort he forced these unwelcome thoughts from his mind, unwilling to sleep with such questions for company, for he knew it led to the turbulence of the soul which the Cardinal could not endure.

✦ ✦

From time to time Cardinal Hetre was plagued with nightmares, and never more than on this night. He tossed on his narrow bed, wishing he were back in Quebec instead of trapped here in Rome, a prisoner of the conclave. Sweat stood out on his brow, his arms thrashed against the sheets as if they were the most formidable bonds. In his dream he screamed and howled, but all that escaped his lips was a soft, pitiful moan.

Something pursued him, something he could not bring himself to face, something that had long ago sent him into the Church for safety, a personal Nemesis more terrible than the promise of Hell for those who sinned. He did not know why he was sought, and had no desire to find out. He wanted only to get away from the terrible thing, and that was the one wish he seemed destined not to be granted.

He sat up in bed and started to pray, quiet, personal petitions to the Virgin and to God for the peace that is not of this world which had eluded him for so long.

✦ ✦

Before the first bells of morning, Charles, Cardinal Mendosa awake. He lay still, staring at the ceiling, wanting to be back in Houston: he hated Rome. Horrible thing for a Catholic to feel, let alone a Cardinal. Rome brought out the worst in him. It was nothing but a monument to its own swollen self-importance, and it colored the Church with grandiose traditions that still made him squirm. He was never more Texan than when he was in Rome.

A month before the conclave, he had received a delegation from the followers of the Reverend Robert Williamson, the most popular of the Fundamentalists preaching the Second Coming on television. The six men were successful and confident, trying to sway the Cardinal to their position in anticipation of the death of Pope Urban IX, who was lying in coma at the Vatican. They presented their statistics and quoted Scripture, making it apparent they expected his cooperation. At the time he had been polite to mask his ire; now he was afraid that those followers of Reverend Williamson might have more strength than he first supposed. They had been so polished. They had told him — very discreetly, of course — that the Church was falling apart and that Reverend Williamson was looking to save the souls of all Christians.

These were not the Protestants Cardinal Mendosa was used to. These men were there to deliver a threat, to put him on notice that they were going to damage him and the Church as much and whenever possible. Never before had Cardinal Mendosa experienced such subtle malice from any Protestants, no matter how angry some of them might have been. Until that interview he had assumed that difficult though it occasionally was, Catholics and Protestants would find some way to rattle along together, their Christianity giving them common ground. After the Reverend Williamson's men visited him, he was no longer certain of it.

Every day the conclave continued gave those slick, dangerous men — and those like them — more power and credibility. Cardinal Mendosa could feel it in the air, even here in Rome. And the dreams had come back. For the first time in almost a decade, he was having those eerie dreams that had brought him into the Church so long ago.

"We're going to have to agree today," he said softly to the darkness. "We don't agree today and this thing's gonna bust wide open." He was not sure he was speaking to anyone other than himself. "If it busts wide open, then it's all over. We'll never get another Pope that everyone can accept." Saying it aloud made him more convinced he was right, casting his thoughts back more than forty years, to the first dreams he had had that had disturbed Father Aloysius, the dear old drunken Irishman who had been his parish priest.

Cardinal Mendosa turned on his side and determinedly closed his eyes, wanting to be rid of the memory. "This is different," he whispered, and saw the dreams again as clearly as he had at nine when he had been examined by Father Aloysius and then Bishop Parker, both men questioning him for hours about what he had seen in his dreams. They had finally dismissed them as the result of the boy's vivid imagination, his vision of a Catholic President shot in Texas while riding in an open car surrounded by police.

And eight years later it happened, exactly as he had dreamed it. Cardinal Mendosa put his hand to his eyes as if that would block what he remembered. The new dreams were as unsettling and as unanswerable, and he found them as hard to turn from now as he had when he was a boy.

"We have to agree. Today," he muttered, shivering in the bed. The new vision dismayed him, and he wanted to be free of it: a Pope who was not Catholic was unthinkable, no matter how theoretically and theologically possible. The Cardinals would have to agree today, or it would be too late.

The first deep bell of Saint Peter's began to toll, a low E that shuddered on the pre-dawn air. Cardinal Mendosa heard it with relief as he threw back the covers and began his first prayers of the morning.

Copyright © 1977 by Paul Mavrides

NON-FICTION REVIEW

Russ Kick

Nazis, Communists, Klansmen, and Others on the Fringe: Political Extremism in America

John George and Laird Wilcox

(Prometheus Books, 1992).

Until this book came out, as far as I am aware, there had never been an objective and comprehensive look at political extremist groups from the far left and the far right. This incredible book finally brings much hard to find information under one cover. Written by two experts in extremism, *Nazis* . . . starts off with a relatively brief look at American extremism from Pre-Columbian days to 1960. It quickly becomes apparent that the authors are ready to call it like they see it: "If one were to describe the Ameri-

can Revolution as a seditious conspiracy fomented by a band of extremists, misfits, malcontents, and troublemakers dedicated to the overthrow of recognized authority, one well might be right on the mark" (p. 16).

Other chapters explore the nature of extremism, why people join (and leave) such movements, and how extremists on both sides of the political spectrum view the rights of those who disagree with them. The meat of the book, though, is Parts Two and Three — an encyclopedic look at the formation, activities, and fate (or current activities) of groups from the extreme left and the extreme right. Far left groups that are covered include the Communist Party USA, Students for a Democratic Society, the Black Panther Party, the Revolutionary Action Movement, and eleven others. Far right groups that are covered include the John Birch Society, the Liberty Lobby, the Minutemen, the Jewish Defense League, neo-Nazi groups, the KKK, and twelve others. Each group gets a chapter of its own. Although the book clocks in at over 500 pages, most of the chapters seem too short, giving at times a cursory look at events. However, this drawback can easily be excused when you look at the book's strong points: there's never a dull moment; the reader gets a strong sense of what these semi-mythical groups really did and what they *really* stood for; and the authors are very objective and have a strong love of freedom of speech and belief.

The book also earns distinction in the way it shows the common threads running through all extremist groups. Namely, the groups' memberships are extremely small, despite their claims to the contrary. They generate an inordinate amount of media coverage, public apprehension, and government harassment. And, when viewed objectively, almost none of them have had any lasting impact upon society.

Nazis . . . ends with a bang. An appendix takes a fascinating look at a favorite tactic of extremists — attributing nonexistent quotes to famous people, and the 47-page (!) annotated bibliography lists enough books on extremism to keep you reading for years.

There has been much written about extremism, but little of it has been comprehensive or without bias. This book corrects this problem and belongs on the shelf of anyone interested in the outermost fringes of politics and society.

Cover-up Lowdown ©'75 BY KINNEY & MAVRIDES

"NO. 399 WITH A BULLET!"

ACCORDING TO THE WARREN COMMISSION, **BULLET "A"** (NO. 399) SHATTERED **2** BONES & CAUSED **7** WOUNDS!

YET **BULLET "B"**, FIRED THRU EQUIVALENT OBSTACLES SHOWS UNIQUELY DIFFERENT **"WEAR & TEAR"**!

Copyright © 1977 by Paul Mavrides and Jay Kinney

BLOOD, SEX AND COMICS

Linda Marotta

Men, Women and Chain Saws: Gender in the Modern Horror Film

Carol J. Clover

(Princeton University Press 260 pp, $19.95)

The tendency of modern horror films to focus on the physical body (and what happens when you open it up) makes them natural sources of meaty material for gender studies. The prevailing public opinion, informed by feminist film theory, assumes that modern slasher films are voyeuristic and misogynistic due to the film makers' male gaze (men look, women are looked at) which forces the audience to view women's bodies fetishistically and take sadistic pleasure in their destruction. Carol Clover, a professor of Scandinavian and Comparative Literature at the University of California at Berkeley, charges not that these films are politically correct, but that they are much more complex (and, yes, even progressive) than the standard male=sadist/fe-male=masochist stereotyping with which they are accused. In this thought-provoking and well argued book, she examines over 200 American horror films from the 1970's to the mid-1980's which most involve issues of gender.

Clover's main argument, that modern horror films experiment with non-traditional gender roles far more often than do mainstream films, is best demonstrated in her analysis of the standard female hero of slasher films whom she dubs the "Final Girl." The assumption that male viewers identify only with male aggressors or saviors, she asserts, is turned around in the horror genre where one encounters a predominantly male audience identifying with a suffering female victim. Digging deeply into films such as *The Texas Chainsaw Massacre II*, *Halloween* and *Alien*, she highlights the masculine characteristics of their anatomically female heroes and the gender confusion that reigns among the killers (usually transvestites or underdeveloped males).

Her examination of other sub-categories also reveal surprising gender-crossing similarities. She finds that occult or possession films such as *Don't Look Now* and *The Exorcist*, generally use the female body as a battleground for the spiritual awakening of a nearby male character. A fascinating chapter on rape revenge films expresses outrage at critics who focus only on the rapists, dismissing the importance of the victim. In her detailed discussion of *I Spit on Your Grave* she charges that "Martin and Porter's [Video Movie Guide: 1987] assessment of the castration scene as 'one of the most appalling moments in cinema history' is itself a pretty appalling testimony to the double standard in matters of sexual violence."

Clover exposes again and again the far greater sexism and repression in mainstream films and points out that successful "breakthrough" films like *Silence of the Lambs*, *The Accused* and *Thelma and Louise* have identical (but safer) plots and messages as low-budget horror films made years ago. This is the best academic treatment of any aspect of the horror genre I have ever read.

Clover addresses many overlooked gaps in gender and film studies, illustrates her arguments engagingly and even takes into account cases that don't neatly fit her theories. If the going gets a little thick in the "sex-gender swamp" (I'm a women identifying as a man identifying as a women, does that make me a lesbian?), it only proves her point. Even readers unfamiliar with concepts such as castration anxiety or the single-sex theory will be amply rewarded by Clover's forays into the city/country dynamic (*The Hills Have Eyes*), female interiority (all those sucking vacuums in *Poltergeist*), meta-

cinematic self-reflection (*Peeping Tom*) and the folkloric aspects of sequels and spin-offs.

Certain to spark controversy, one hopes her book will inspire further studies in this popular and psychologically fertile genre. Her generalization of the audience as male dominated is understandable, but it made me yearn for a treatment that includes us "invisible" female spectators and fans.

Jeffrey Dahmer: An Unauthorized Biography of a Serial Killer

Hart D. Fisher, writer; Al Hanford, artist

(Boneyard Press, $2.50)

The Further Adventures of Young Jeffrey Dahmer

Eric Gneof, artist/writer

(Boneyard Press, $2.75)

Amateurish in every way, this badly drawn, ungrammatical dramatization of Dahmer's career gained so much negative publicity that it precipitated a lawsuit by five of Dahmer's victims' families and a protest march to publisher Fisher's house! The cops suggested he get out of town, so he held a backyard barbecue. Riled up, he made the second book a total gross-out shocker. Drawn in a fittingly funny/grotesque style, it features Dahmer's hideous birth, a young Dan Quayle and child molesters Clinton and Bush. Pretty retarded stuff, but the second half of the comic reproduced some amazing photos of the protest march.

Screw Comics #1

Edited by Kevin Hein and Sue Nock

(Eros Comix, $3.50)

Little did we know that nestled among the snatches in *Screw* are a shit load of outrageous comics from some of the hottest underground cartoonists around. In case you've missed any issues, you can now catch a peek at strips that Danny Hellman, Peter Bagge, Spain, Kaz and Steve Cerio probably didn't show to their parents. From Cerio's trippy "flying homo ghosts" to John T. Quinn III's Calvin and Hobbes/Oedipus Rex parody to Kaz's "Brown Eye, the Sailor" you'll find more shit, come and big veiny dicks in this hilarious comic book than you'll ever find sticking to the inside of Al Goldstein's undershorts.

ST ET SMA T : FICTION REVIEWS

Anthony Alcaraz

Shella
Andrew Vachss
Knopf, $20

In blasting Andrew Vachss' new novel *Shella,* one critic bemoaned the fact that Vachss had — at least for one book — abandoned his street-wise, street-tough, take-no-prisoners avenging angel Burke; Vachss' protagonist in his critically acclaimed series of suspense novels. Burke's the guy you'd want on your side if you were in trouble, but you'd have to count the silverware if you had him over for dinner. If you weren't one of "his" people he'd run a scam by you and leave you destitute without an ounce of remorse as an abject lesson.

But Burke goes after pedophiles; the most loathsome of creatures, and regardless of Burke's methods and disdain for the laws of society, he is far better than his prey; hence a sympathetic figure. He is, moreover, surrounded by a colorful cast of characters, full of breadth and depth; "good" people one and all.

While Burke's many fans crave his return (and return he will, I am told, with Vachss' next novel), no one should criticize Vachss for branching out. Robert Parker may be content with writing his Spenser novels the rest of his life, but no one should condemn an author for wanting to break the mold.

That *Shella* does not succeed does not mean Vachss is a failure without Burke as his vehicle. Most fans are unaware Vachss has written reams of short stories; tight, taut, wonderfully told and crafted — all without Burke. Many have been adapted into comics by Dark Horse in his *Hard Looks* series, and it would behoove true Vachss fans to check them out at your local comic store.

One also has to wonder if *Shella* was written as a true departure from his Burke novels or is just another example of the author's need for total control. Vachss reportedly told his publisher he would only write another Burke novel if they published *Shella.* Vachss, much like Burke, pushes the envelope at every opportunity. He sees how far he can go and then demands more. He sold the rights to *Blue Belle* (a Burke novel) and in a Dark Horse interview said he hopes the film is never made. Why? He doesn't have complete creative control and would be disappointed in some way, shape or form regardless of how well the film was made.

So Knopf wants a Burke novel in the worst way; Burke's legion of fans has grown with each book, due in great part to word of mouth. Those who read Vachss for the first time are caught hook, line and sinker and become addicted. Vachss tells his publisher, sure, if you publish *Shella* first. One can only imagine the apoplexy suffered by the suits at Knopf when they saw the finished product. Not that *Shella* is a terrible book, but if the Burke series is dark, *Shella* is bleaker still; the darkest shade of black — and one not likely to garner additional admirers.

The main character, Ghost, is Burke without a conscience. He kills on command. Where Burke hunts pedophiles, Ghost kills as its the path of least resistance.

The plot of simple. Ghost has gone to prison, having killed while saving his girlfriend. Ghost gets out of prison and can't locate his girlfriend. Ghost does the bidding (always involving killing) for those who will help lead him to his elusive girlfriend. Along with way Ghost meets a whole host of characters, most just as despicable as him. For the most part they are stereotypes; cardboard, two-dimensional figures completely unlike those Burke surrounds himself with or encounters. Lack of characterization is the books weakest link.

This isn't to say *Shella* is not well-written. It is typical Vachss stylistically; short and sparse without an unnecessary word or sentence. When Ghost gets into a car or jeep, it is just that; a car or a jeep with maybe the color added for description. It is a quick read, even if ultimately an unsatisfying one.

One gets the feeling there is a lot of Burke in Vachss. As an attorney dealing with cases involving abused children, one can see Vachss possibly stepping over the line that separates what is legal to save an abused child. The end justifies the means. In *Shella*, Vachss wanted to flex his muscles with his publisher. He held firm; they blinked. Another scam a success. As much as this reviewer craves the Burke series, it is hoped Vachss will continue to push the envelope with future non-Burke novels. Such books, though, should build upon the strengths of the Burke series; well-crafted, colorful, 3-dimensional characters that is the hallmark of his best work.

Winter Prey
John Sandford
Putnam, $21.95

Lucas Davenport is back in John Sandford's "Prey" series; sorry to say the least satisfying to date. Davenport, the former Minneapolis cop, has quit the force though he is not enjoying his "retirement." He is asked to aid a small Wisconsin town besieged by the Iceman, who's just laid waste to a family of three.

The problems here are many. After four books, Sandford adds no depth to his protagonist (as opposed to Vachss' Burke who is constantly emerging). As always

Davenport gets entangled with a woman; this time one stalked by the Iceman. (Real-life cops and private eyes should have it so good. Seems Davenport can't sneeze without a woman wanting to jump his bones.) The Iceman, menacingly drawn out the outset quickly disintegrates, killing suspects and witnesses alike to cover his tracks. Worst of all, as a whodunnit, the books fails miserably. When the perp is unmasked, the reader can only scratch his head; no clues, no foreshadowing. A overly long drawn out (and needlessly bloody) chase follows and one doesn't have to be a genius to guess the outcome.

Either Sandford must reinvent Davenport or put the character to bed. *Winter Prey* will most definitely leave readers cold.

L.A. Times
Stuart Woods
HarperCollins, $21.00

Unlike Sandford, Stuart Woods' novels are eminently readable, can't-put-down page turners; even when he's not at his best. L.A. *Times* is light fare for Woods, but engaging and well worth the read, nevertheless. *Publishers Weekly*, in reviewing the book refers to Woods as a "pro-

lific crime writer," but that description sells him woefully short. Woods, like few other novelists, has successfully navigated every genre. Under the Lake was a superb novel of horror; *Palindrome* great suspense; *Grass Roots* and *Chiefs* knock-em-dead tales of political intrigue.

In L.A. *Times,* Vincente Callabrese is a mafia underling who loves films, — really loves films — wants to make movies; ultimately does. Along the way he uses and abuses an array of wonderfully drawn characters. An admitted sociopath, he leaves devastation in his wake in his climb to the top as a Hollywood movie mogul.

As Michael Vincent, Callabrese makes use of his former-mafia contacts when necessary and his life becomes increasingly complicated. Who gets the upper hand in this roller coaster ride is what makes L.A. *Times* tick.

Vincent/Callabrese is a heavily layered complex character who can both repulse and enthrall the reader in the same chapter; no, on the same page. A great read, L.A. *Times* hopefully will turn readers on to Woods' other books; in which case a real treat is in store.

Anthony Alcaraz, Gauntlet's new fiction reviewer, is from New England

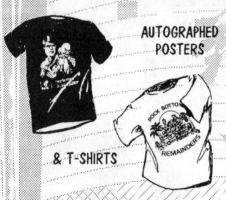

THE LAST GASP CATALOG

YOUR SOURCE FOR EROTIC MATERIAL OF ALL STYLES

Over twenty years of experience in the distribution of adult entertainment from the mainstream to the fringes

Brilliant theorists meet talented graphic artists in the Last Gasp Catalog, a thick quarterly catalog offering a choice of erotica from all sources. *Bright, Califia, Dworkin, Foucault, Baudrillard and Paglia meet DeSade, Rice, Bataille, Crumb, Manara & Stanton.*

Magazines of all opinions and horizons cover news of the reporting and writing worlds. *Bad Attitude, Libido, Yellow Silk, Girljock, Rubberist, SkinTwo*